God's Willing Knowledge

GOD'S WILLING KNOWLEDGE

The Influence of Scotus' Analysis of Omniscience

Douglas C. Langston

THE PENNSYLVANIA STATE
UNIVERSITY PRESS
UNIVERSITY PARK AND LONDON

To David Wall Langston, Jr.
_____

Library of Congress Cataloging-in-Publication Data

Langston, Douglas C.
    God's willing knowledge.

    Includes index.
    1. God—Omniscience—History of doctrines—Middle
Ages, 600–1500.   2. Duns Scotus, John, ca. 1266–1308—
Contributions in theology.   I. Title.
BT131.L36 1986   231'.4   85–31956
ISBN 0-271-00429-0

Contents

God's Willing Knowledge

Introduction

The philosophers and theologians of the Age of Faith wrestled with issues concerning free will and determinism, and they exercised considerable skill and imagination in attempting to resolve them. They not only discussed, with great insight, the problems of causal determinism and the difficulties in ascribing truth value to sentences about the future, but, in addition, they pondered yet another form of determinism: whether God's omniscience determines all events in the world. Although contemporary thinkers have addressed this issue, the attention given it between the fourth and the seventeenth centuries remains unequalled.

Certain of the issues connected with God's omniscience are familiar to most of us: Does God know the future by knowing the determinate truth values of sentences about the future? Does God set up mechanical sequences in the world that cause certain events to take place? Other issues are less familiar: Does God know events in the world by observing them, or in some other way? If God is omniscient, can he hold a false belief? If God's omniscience precludes free will, what becomes of man's moral responsibility? What is the relationship between God's omniscience and the fact that evil exists in the world?

Many thinkers have, of course, attempted to deal with this complicated set of questions. The discussions of Boethius and Aquinas, for example, have helped to delineate the problems surrounding God's omniscience. From these men we have inherited the striking assumption that God's knowledge is somehow separable from the activities of his will. This emphasis has caused many subsequent thinkers to approach the relationship between God's omniscience and human freedom as a problem chiefly of the logic of the word 'know'.

Yet, many have rejected this assumption. Indeed, some of the most important contributors to questions of God's omniscience and related issues have believed God's knowledge to be intimately related to the activities of his will. This second tradition, which I call the voluntarist tradition because of its emphasis on the activities of God's will, has by contrast been largely neglected. Many people today understand Aquinas' view of God's omniscience, but few could recount the basic points of this second, equally important, tradition. My aim, then, in the present essay is to discuss the voluntarist tradition, and to focus particularly upon the doctrines of its founding father, Duns Scotus.

John Duns Scotus (1265–1308) is widely acknowledged as one of the most important philosopher-theologians of the Middle Ages. Yet, Scotus' doctrines, when compared to the arguments of such men as Aquinas and Anselm, are little known and poorly understood. This was not always the case. During and immediately following his lifetime, Scotus was widely discussed, and his doctrines served as starting points for further inquiry. His influence pervaded philosophical circles even outside the Church well into the seventeenth century. Especially important was his analysis of God's omniscience. His delineation of this complex issue—particularly his insistence that God's knowledge is inextricably connected to his will—informed the network of assumptions of many subsequent thinkers.

Modern neglect of Scotus can be attributed to the abstruseness of his doctrines. This difficulty—which earned him the title "The Subtle Doctor" among admirers and caused detractors to use his name to coin the pejorative term "dunce"—is understandably daunting to those not specializing in medieval philosophy. Even specialists in medieval thought find much of Scotus' writings confusing.

One of my chief desires in this book is to clarify and evaluate Scotus' views on omniscience, freedom, and related issues. This is important not only for understanding Scotus himself, but also for understanding those who followed him and inherited his assumptions. Many of the most important writers about the relationship between God's omniscience and human freedom—Molina, Luther, Calvin, Hobbes, Leibniz—presuppose much of what is found in Scotus' writings on the problem, and their discussions can be clarified by seeing their indebtedness to him.

I am indebted in many ways to many people for this book. Marilyn Adams, Robert Adams, and Eleonore Stump gave useful criticisms and timely suggestions on various parts of the book. Mike Michalson was the first person to read the whole manuscript in its initial form and his encouragement was essential to the project. Dale Ballou, John Murdoch, and Bill Graham were helpful ears during my stay at Harvard. Calvin Normore was an inexhaustible source of criticism and encouragement. I owe a great debt to Nelson Pike for reading several early drafts, teaching me what clarity of writing and thinking is, and for his patience during my graduate years. Jeffrey Stout brought my manuscript to the attention of The Pennsylvania State University Press and Philip Winsor of the Press shepherded the manuscript through its obstacles. Norma Singleton receives great thanks for typing the manuscript into a word processor. My greatest thanks is to Constance Whitesell who encouraged, cajoled, edited, and typed.

I also wish to thank the Mellon Faculty Fellowship Program and the Committee On The Study Of Religion of Harvard University for the year of support (1980–81) when the original draft was completed; Leverett House, Harvard University (especially the Andrewses) for its hospitality; and the Division of Sponsored Research of the University of South Florida for its crucial financial support during the summer of 1981.

Part I
Scotus' Doctrine

1 Scotus' Analysis of God's Omniscience

INTRODUCTION

God, according to medieval thought, is omniscient, that is, he knows all that is knowable. To most medieval thinkers, this means both that God knows the past and the present, and also that he can know the future. That is to say, he can know the truth value of such sentences as: "Mount St. Helens will erupt in 1990" and "Socrates will run in the race tomorrow."

Both of these sentences concern events that may or may not occur. Mount St. Helens might or might not erupt in 1990; Socrates might run in tomorrow's race, or he might decide not to run. Such sentences describe future events that are contingent, as their occurrence is not logically necessary. Consequently, they are called "future contingent sentences."

Medieval philosophers, however, detected a problem in God's knowledge of future contingents: If God knows, for example, that Mount St. Helens will erupt in 1990, then Mount St. Helens must erupt in 1990. That is, if God knows that it will erupt in 1990, it is necessary that it erupt, which implies that Mount St. Helens' eruption is not contingent.

This difficulty is not easily resolved. Proponents of main-stream Western Christianity cannot simply assert that, even though God knows that some future contingent will occur, it might not occur. For in such a case, a belief God holds to be true would prove false, so that God would hold a false belief. If God is omniscient, as mainstream Christianity believes him to be, it is logically impossible for him to hold a false belief.[1] Thus, apparently, all that God knows about the future must occur. His knowledge of future contingents, therefore, seems to render them no longer contingent.

Several medieval philosophers attempted to reconcile God's knowledge of future contingents with their contingency. Abelard does so in his *Logica Ingredientibus* by arguing that there is a sense in which something other than what God fore-knows can happen. Lombard in the *Sentences* solves the difficulty by saying that God could have known other than he knows. Robert Grosseteste in *De Libero Arbitrio* attacks the problem by distinguishing between necessity and immutability.[2] The best known solution, however, is that advanced by Thomas Aquinas, which involves certain claims about God's intellect and an appeal to God's existing outside time. Much the same solution had been advanced by Boethius and Anselm, and in his presentation of the solution Aquinas draws distinctions similar to those made by Abelard, Lombard, and Grosseteste. Never-theless, subsequent generations have regarded it as Aquinas' solution.

John Duns Scotus, writing twenty-five years after Aquinas' death, also dealt with the problem of future contingents. He offered a solution differing from that of Aquinas, Anselm, and Boethius by strongly emphasizing the role of God's will in his knowledge. He came to this analysis not only because he saw God's will as his primary faculty, but also because he found his predecessors' solutions unsatisfactory. Although Scotus' solu-tion seems decidedly idiosyncratic, as we shall see later, it has nevertheless been studied and appropriated by subsequent phi-losophers and theologians dealing with the problems of God's omniscience.

In this chapter, I shall explain Scotus' solution to the problem of God's knowledge of future contingents. Since Scotus' solution represents a reaction to the difficulties he perceived in the solution posed by Aquinas, I shall also present this solution and discuss Scotus' objections to it.

AQUINAS' ANALYSIS OF OMNISCIENCE

Aquinas discusses the relationship between God's omniscience and the contingency of events in several places.[3] Of particular interest is the discussion in the *Commentary on the Sentences,* Book I, distinction 38, question 1, article 5, for it presents the intricacies of his position in a particularly revealing way.

The discussion follows the usual format of sentence commentaries. First the question—whether God has knowledge of future contingents—is posed. Seven arguments that he does not are then presented. There is the presentation of the statement for the opinion and then the *responsio* section in which Aquinas gives his own answer to the question. Finally, Aquinas replies to the original seven arguments in the last section of the article. Most of the important philosophical points made are to be found in his responses to the objections, especially in the discussion centering around objections three and four.

Objection three begins in this way: The objector assumes that God knows that Socrates is running. The objector then points out that it is either possible or impossible for Socrates not to run. Now, to claim that it is impossible for Socrates not to run entails that he runs by necessity, which means that Socrates' running is not contingent. On the other hand, if it is possible for Socrates not to run, a difficulty of another sort presents itself. Suppose he does not run. Then God, who by assumption knows that Socrates is running, knows a falsehood. God would not, under these circumstances, be omniscient. But since God is omniscient, it follows that, if God knows that Socrates is running, Socrates must run, i.e., his running is neither free nor contingent.

This argument reveals what is at the root of the conflict between God's omniscience and the contingency of human actions. If God is essentially omniscient, it is not logically possible for God to know that some p occur and that p not occur. This argument pertains specifically to a present-tense sentence, viz., "Socrates is running," but the argument clearly applies as well to a past-tense sentence. That is, if we were to change the example so that at some time in the past God knew that Socrates will run, we have the same problem. It would be logically impossible for God to have known that some p occur, and that p not occur. Indeed, this is part of the position represented in the fourth objection in which Aquinas discusses the sentence "Socrates runs, if this was foreknown by God."[4]

Aquinas discusses a number of issues in order to disarm these objections. According to him, it is clear that the central difficulty is in how one understands the sentence "what is known by God necessarily is true."[5] Those who claim that God's knowledge is necessitating usually interpret the sentence in a *de re* way (also called "the necessity of the consequent"), which may be paraphrased as: "If something is known by God, it is necessary." Given this reading, whatever God knows is necessary, and so lacks any contingency. God's omniscience is therefore inconsistent with the contingency of events.

As Aquinas points out, however, there is an alternative reading to the sentence, a *de dicto* reading (also called the "necessity of the inference"), which may be paraphrased as: "Necessarily, if something is known by God, it is true." It is interesting that this reading affirms that, if something is known by God, it cannot be false, without implying that what is known by God is itself necessary. That is, given that God knows something, it is certain that what he knows is true. But it does not follow that what he knows to be true had to be true; it could have happened that it is false even though it is in fact true.

Aquinas correctly argues that anyone concerned with disproving necessitation through God's omniscience must give the sentence "what is known by God necessarily is true" a *de dicto* interpretation.[6] Those arguing that God's knowledge entails necessitation argue that it is God's knowledge of an event that necessitates the event. So the problem lies in the relationship between the event and God's knowledge of it. This relationship is not, however, captured by the *de re* reading of "what is known by God necessarily is true," for this reading affirms that the event God knows is itself necessary. But if it is necessary, the event will occur under any possible circumstances. It will occur *even if* God believes that it will not occur. Thus, the claim that it is God's knowledge that necessitates an event is lost on the *de re* reading. Only the *de dicto* reading captures the idea that it is the relationship between God's foreknowledge and the occurrence (or non-occurrence) of an event that seems to necessitate the occurrence (or non-occurrence) of the event.

As Aquinas realizes, however, merely advocating the *de dicto* reading of "what is known by God necessarily is true" does not eliminate the problem of necessitation through God's omniscience. Even on the *de dicto* reading, if God's knowledge is itself necessary, then the event he knows is necessary as well.

As many have pointed out, God's knowledge can itself be necessary in two ways: if it is in the past, or if it is immutable.[7] The pastness of God's knowledge would render it necessary in the sense that, once God knew something, his knowledge could not be otherwise since, logically speaking, the past cannot be changed. Thus, if God knew yesterday that Socrates will run in the race the day after tomorrow, it would be necessary that Socrates run then, since the knowledge God had yesterday is in the past, which cannot change. Similarly, if God's knowledge is immutable in the sense that what he knows is the only thing he could know, his knowledge would be necessary and all that he knew would be necessary. Before dealing with these various points and answering objections three and four, Aquinas offers an overview of his theory of God's omniscience in the *responsio* section of his discussion. This overview provides the basis for his answers to the objections.

In the *responsio* section, Aquinas claims that from eternity God knows each contingent. What he means is that God, in one, simultaneous, non-successive, and timeless act, knows each and every contingent in its determinate existence. For Aquinas, this implies two things. First of all, it implies that God and his cognitions, existing in eternity, are present to each contingent in its own determinate existence. It also implies that each and every contingent in its determinate existence is present to God. From these two claims it follows that God does not have foreknowledge in the sense that he knows before something occurs that it will occur. Since all contingents are present to him, he knows them only as present.[8] Importantly, God does not know these contingents by directly intuiting them. According to Aquinas, this would imply some lack in God, i.e., that God needed something other than himself. God knows contingents by seeing likenesses of the contingents in his divine essence. He also knows through his essence contingents that never exist since he can see in his essence his power to make these non-existents actual (even though he never does actualize them).[9]

Given that what God knows is present to him, the problems surrounding the contingency of events disappear. To see this, we need only examine the case of Socrates running. That Socrates runs when he runs is something that is certain and necessary. Moreover, anyone who sees Socrates run can be certain that he is running since it is not possible that one knows that he is running and he not be running. But the knowledge of the running does not determine the running. The running is a contingent event, and it is thus possible that Socrates not run. If he were not to run, of course, one observing Socrates would know that he is not running. So the fact that future contingents are present to God guarantees that God can know them with certainty in a non-necessitating fashion. The position put forth in the *responsio* section thus provides a ready reply to objection three. Socrates' running is present to God as temporally present events are present to us. Our knowledge of these events is certain and necessary, but our knowledge does not make the events themselves necessary. In a similar way, God's knowledge of Socrates' running is certain and necessary, but it does not render Socrates' running necessary.

The position also answers the fourth objection. Since God's knowledge is outside time, one cannot claim that God's knowledge is in the past relative to any event. Thus God does not foreknow what occurs. On the contrary, he knows what occurs because the occurrence is present to him. Hence, there is no necessitation of an event by virtue of God's knowledge being in the past relative to that event.

Moreover, there is no necessitation of events because of the immutability of God's knowledge. Since God's knowledge is present to events like Socrates' running, given that Socrates runs, God would know this, and it can never be the case that he not know it. But this does not mean that Socrates could not refrain from running. Had he so refrained, God would know this and then this knowledge would be immutable.

Aquinas' discussion of God's omniscience in his *Commentary on the Sentences* is philosophically rich. He makes distinctions that are extremely important for clarifying the relationship between God's knowledge and events in the world. But in general, Aquinas' solution to the problem of necessitation through God's knowledge is a dissolution of the problem. Since God's knowledge is present to the future contingents he knows and these future contingents are present to God, there is no foreknowledge and, consequently, no necessitation.

SCOTUS' ANALYSIS OF GOD'S OMNISCIENCE

In *Ordinatio,* Book I, distinction 38, part two, and distinction 39, questions one to five, Scotus explains how God knows future contingents.[10] Like Aquinas' analysis, Scotus' analysis is given in the context of arguments that God cannot have knowledge of contingents. In fact, Scotus presents five different types of arguments for this negative claim at the beginning of the second part of Book I, distinction 38, and then replies to these arguments at the end of distinction 39. In his response to these arguments, he makes a number of points very similar to those made by Aquinas. For example, Scotus affirms that the problem of God's knowledge of events must be formulated in terms of the necessity of inference and not in terms of the necessity of the consequent since God can know other than he does know.[11] Scotus also points out that immutability must be distinguished from logical necessity. For while it is true that once something is posited about God it cannot be otherwise, it is not true that whatever is posited about God was the only thing that could have been posited.[12] Despite the similarities in their analyses, Scotus' solution to the problem of God's knowledge of contingents differs considerably from Aquinas'.

Scotus presents his solution in two parts: First he explains how there are contingencies; then he indicates how this explanation of contingency is consistent with the certainty and immutability of God's knowledge of contingents. According to Scotus, there is an essential order of causes for every effect in the universe.[13] Moreover, all essential orders of causes are ordered to one cause, God. So, according to Scotus, God's activity sustains every chain of co-existing causes and co-causes all the effects of every essential order of causes. Since Scotus equates "being contingent" with "having been caused contingently," it follows, according to Scotus, that there can be contingents only if God causes contingently.[14] If God necessarily produces whatever he produces, all the essential orders of causes would be orders of necessary causes and there would be no contingent causes or effects. Since it is obvious that there are contingents,[15] it follows that God causes contingently. Thus, on Scotus' analysis, there are contingents because there are some things God has caused that he could logically have refrained from producing. In addition, since Scotus thinks that God's intellect is a natural agent (i.e., a non-voluntary agent that has no control over its function), he locates the source of contingency in God's will. Consequently, according to Scotus, there are contingencies because God could will into existence other things than those he in fact wills into existence. Scotus explains in great detail how God could will other things than he in fact wills, and I shall address his remarks in the next chapter. Let us now, however, turn to the second part of his analysis: how God certainly and immutably knows contingents.

Since Scotus claims that all occurrences are co-caused by God's will, it is not surprising that he sees the activity of God's will as an important part of God's knowledge of contingents. According to Scotus, in the eternal now the divine intellect presents to the divine will all possible states of affairs. Out of all these possibilities, the divine will chooses one possible consistent set to exist in willed existence. The divine intellect then grasps the determination of the divine will. Since Scotus believes that whatever the divine will causes to exist in willed existence necessarily comes to exist in actual existence, Scotus concludes that the divine intellect knows with certainty what states of affairs exist in actual existence. Of course, these states of affairs are contingent even though they are known with certainty since God could will into willed existence some other consistent set of contingents. In this manner, according to Scotus, God can have certain and immutable knowledge of future contingents.[16]

Scotus' answer to the question of how God can have certain and immutable knowledge of future contingents is thus very simple. The divine will causes contingently whatever it brings about because it could bring into willed existence some consistent set of occurrences other than the one set it in fact does.[17] Once the divine will brings about a certain consistent set of occurrences in willed existence, this set necessarily exists in actual existence. Since the divine intellect knows the determination of the divine will, it thus knows certainly and immutably what future contingents will in fact exist. Having now briefly viewed Scotus' theory, let us examine the difficulties with Aquinas' analysis that led Scotus to formulate his theory in such a way. This examination will also reveal further aspects of Scotus' own theory.

SCOTUS' OBJECTIONS TO AQUINAS' ANALYSIS

Scotus did not regard his analysis of God's knowledge as a mere alternative to Aquinas' analysis. On the contrary, he offered a different explanation because he found two major difficulties

with Aquinas' position. The first is that Aquinas' analysis collapses the differences among past, present, and future. The
second is that it fails to account adequately for God's knowledge
of many actual events. As we shall see, the first problem is explicitly presented in the text of *Ordinatio,* Book I, distinction 39.
The second problem, which is presented only implicitly in this
text, is the more important of the two.

After stating the questions for and against the claim that God
has knowledge of contingents, Scotus treats, in *Ordinatio,*
Book I, distinction 39, three solutions offered by various philosophers to the attendant difficulties. The second opinion is that
of Aquinas, which Scotus characterizes in this way: "Some
assume that God has certain knowledge of future contingents
for the different reason that the whole flux of time and everything that is in time is present to eternity."[18] His response to
this position is very clear:

> Again, if an effect has existence in itself in relation to the
> first cause, it absolutely exists in itself, since there is
> nothing in relation to which it could have a more real
> existence. Thus, what is said to be such in relation to the
> first cause, can be said to be such absolutely. Therefore, if
> something future is actual in relation to God, it is abso-
> lutely actual. Therefore, it is impossible that it should be
> made actual later.
>
> Further, if my future sitting—not only insofar as it has
> knowledge of existence—is now present to eternity, then
> it is now produced in that existence by God. For nothing
> has existence in the flux of time from God unless it is
> produced by God according to that existence. But God
> will produce that sitting, or the soul of the Antichrist—
> the situation is the same. Therefore, what has already
> been produced by Him, will be produced in existence
> again and so will be twice produced in existence.[19]

The point Scotus is stressing is that something is present to
God only if it exists. Thus, if I am writing these words on
August 20, 1983, and this is present to God, and I shall be
teaching a class on September 15, 1989, and this is present to
God, my future teaching must also exist on August 20, 1983.
But if it exists on August 20, 1983, it cannot begin to exist at
some future time, viz., September 15, 1989. So Aquinas' theory

implies that nothing can begin to exist in the future. This, of course, is an absurd consequence.[20]

Aquinas seems to have anticipated this type of objection and tried to answer it in the *Summa Contra Gentiles*, Book I, chapter 67, by offering the following analogy: Aquinas suggests that we think of a center of a circle and the points on the circumference of the circle. It is clear the various points on the circumference will be present to the center just as the center will be present to the points. If we think of God as analogous to the center and the various points of time as analogous to the points on the circumference, we can understand how God can be present to all of time and all of time be present to God.

Scotus discusses this illustration at the end of *Ordinatio*, Book I, distinction 39. He regards the illustration as ineffective for this reason: In order for all of the points on the circumference to be simultaneously present to the center, all the points must exist simultaneously. Since the points on the circumference are intended to correspond to the different points of time—past, present, and future—it would follow that, in order for the different points of time to be present to God, they must exist simultaneously. But then past, present, and future would all be present. This, of course, is contradictory.

So, Scotus' first objection to Aquinas' analysis is that the condition that all points of time be present to God collapses the difference among past, present, and future. In general, if a time in the past and a time in the future are both present to God, they must both exist at the same time. So, the distinctions among past, present, and future are obliterated.

There is, of course, an obvious criticism of Scotus' argument. A defender of Aquinas can argue that Scotus fails to make an important distinction. He fails to distinguish "present to something temporal" from "present to something eternal."[21] It is true to say that event$_1$—Socrates will run—and event$_2$—Socrates was sitting—must occur at the same instant of time, e.g., t$_3$, if they were both present to the same temporal event$_3$—Socrates is sitting. If, however, event$_1$ and event$_2$ are present to something that is eternal, they need not occur at the same instant of time. Once this distinction is admitted, Scotus' criticism fails. Of course, Scotus would probably be unwilling to admit such a distinction, especially given the failure of Aquinas' analogy with the circle. Whether Scotus is justified in the rejection is debatable, but it does seem that the burden of proof to justify such a distinction is on Aquinas.

It is worth noting, however, that Scotus' own analysis of omniscience escapes his first criticism of Aquinas' position. On Scotus' analysis, God directly knows things as they exist in willed existence, and willed existence is very different from actual existence. For example, willed existence is timeless and occurs in God's essence; actual existence, on the other hand, is in time and is outside God's essence. Thus all that exists in willed existence can be simultaneous and the actual counterparts, found in temporal time, can occur at different times. The certainty of God's knowledge of what is in time, as Scotus points out, rests on the fact that what God wills in willed existence must come about in actual existence.

Although Scotus' first criticism of Aquinas' analysis of omniscience is less than compelling, his second general criticism is of a different nature. Scotus regards God's intellect as a nonvoluntary agent. Its function is to know everything knowable, and it has no control over this. For Scotus this means that the divine intellect naturally knows through the divine essence all possible states of affairs. Indeed, in his discussions of the divine intellect, he claims that, in the first instant of nature of the divine intellect, all possible states of affairs are found in the divine essence.[22]

The possible states of affairs in the divine intellect fall into one of two categories. The first category consists of those possible states of affairs that may or may not become actual. Of themselves, they carry no mark of their actuality. The second category consists of those possibilities that must obtain, e.g., the logical truths. So, the divine intellect in its first instant of nature does not know which contingent possibilities are to be actual. It knows only that those possibilities that must obtain are to be actual, and these are not contingent possibilities. It thus cannot, by its own power, know all that is to be actual. According to Scotus, the divine intellect requires the divine will to determine which contingent possibilities are to be actual. In the second instant of nature, the divine will chooses some consistent set of contingent possibilities and causes this complex set to become actual. This set plus the possibilities that must obtain constitute the universe as we know it. Thus, until the divine will chooses one set of contingent possibilities over all the others, the divine intellect cannot know which set—of all the contingent possibilities it knows—is to be actual. Consequently, according to Scotus, a purely intellectualistic analysis of omniscience that fails to take into account the activity of the divine will cannot explain God's knowledge of contingent events. Only an analysis involving the divine will is sufficient to explain God's knowledge.[23]

This position suggests a compelling critique of Aquinas' analysis as presented in his *Commentary on the Sentences.* If we return to this analysis, we recall that Aquinas thought that God knows existing contingents through likenesses found in his essence.[24] Aquinas is not, however, clear about how these likenesses are present in the divine essence. There seem to be two possible explanations. On the one hand, God might cause the likenesses to be present in his essence. If this is so, God must somehow guarantee that what he wills to be in his essence have corresponding real counterparts in the world. If he did not, what God knows through his essence about the world might not correspond to the actual world, and God would, consequently, hold false beliefs. On the other hand, God's essence might act like a mirror and naturally reflect those actualities found in the world. The likenesses would be found in God's essence by reflecting the actualities in the world. This would, of course, guarantee that God does not hold false beliefs about the world. Nevertheless, there is a difficulty with this view: How is it that the actualities exist in the world so as to be reflected in the divine essence? Do these actualities simply exist, or are they willed to exist by God? Given what Aquinas claims about God's power (i.e., everything that exists, exists by God's power), Aquinas must think that the actualities in the world exist and are reflected in God's essence only because God wills them to exist in the world.

It is clear that either explanation involves the activity of God's will. On the first option, God must will the likenesses to be marked to indicate that they have real counterparts in the world, and he must guarantee through the activities of his will that these counterparts exist. On the second option, he must will the actualities to exist so that the relevant likenesses exist in his essence and are known by the divine intellect. Scotus, I think, saw that on Aquinas' analysis the divine intellect *qua* natural agent would know only possibilities unless its activity is connected with the activity of the divine will. To avoid this difficulty, in his own analysis of God's omniscience, he made the activity of the divine will essential for the divine knowledge of existing contingents.

It is possible, however, that Scotus overstates his disagreement with Aquinas. In certain passages in his discussions of God's omniscience, Aquinas appears to be aware that the activity of the divine will is essential for divine knowledge. For example, in *Summa Theologiae,* Question 13, article 9, Aquinas says:

> . . . God's knowledge is the cause of things when the will is joined [to it]. Hence, it is not right that whatever God knows is, was, or will be. Only those that he wills to be or permits to be [are, were, or will be]. Moreover, it is not in the knowledge of God that these are, but only that they can be.[25]

There are similar passages in the *Summa Contra Gentiles,*[26] indicating that Aquinas agrees with Scotus that the divine will must play an essential role in God's knowledge of certain contingents. These passages, however, occur along with other passages that downplay the role of God's willing activity in his knowledge.[27]

Various scholars have noted the tension between these sets of passages and have explained it as an outcome of the developing role of practical knowledge in Aquinas' thought.[28] In his earliest writings and especially in his *Commentary on the Sentences,* Aquinas analyzed God's knowledge as a function of his speculative knowledge. Purely intellectualistic, this type of knowledge presents God's knowledge through metaphors of vision: God sees in his essence the objects he knows. God's willing activity has no importance for this type of knowledge, for at this stage in his writing Aquinas emphasizes the difference between the activities of the will and the intellect in God.

In his later writings like *De Veritate, Summa Theologiae,* and *Summa Contra Gentiles,* Aquinas tended to stress the connections between the intellect and the will and began to emphasize God's practical knowledge. Borrowed from Aristotle, this type of knowledge is closely joined by Aquinas to God's causality. In fact, he often speaks of God's practical knowledge as coextensive with his causality and frequently uses metaphors of a craftsman and his art to explain this type of knowledge. Aquinas uses practical knowledge to explain how God knows particulars:

> The difference between speculative and practical knowl-
> edge is that speculative knowledge and what is connected
> without is perfected in the universal, whereas what per-
> tains to practical knowledge is perfected in the particular.
> For the end of speculative knowledge is truth, which
> consists first and of its very nature in the immaterial and
> universal; whereas the end of practical knowledge is
> operation, which is about individual things.[29]

Since knowledge of particulars falls under God's omniscience, it
is clear that God's practical knowledge plays a role in God's
knowledge of future contingents. That is to say, God is the
efficient cause of individual actions and events and thus knows
them as their cause. Thus, if we take into account Aquinas'
comments about practical knowledge, he did emphasize the role
of God's willing in his knowledge and Scotus' second criticism
of Aquinas seems misguided.

It is unfortunate that Scotus' explicit comments on Aquinas'
analysis of omniscience are few and leave many questions
unanswered. The little that Scotus says suggests that he sees
Aquinas as presenting God's omniscience as purely a form of
speculative knowledge. This is, however, an uncharitable view
of Scotus as student of Aquinas. Surely Scotus was aware of
Aquinas' emphasis on the importance of God's will in creation
and providence. If we grant this knowledge to Scotus, we should
attribute to him a much more sophisticated treatment of Aquinas'
views. Moreover, given Scotus' emphasis on human freedom
(which will be treated in the next chapter), we can see his
divergence from Aquinas as centering around human freedom.
(Indeed, Molina and others regard this as one of the key differences between Aquinas and Scotus.) Taking these issues into
consideration and at the risk of historical inaccuracy, I believe
we can best understand Scotus' criticism of Aquinas in this way.

According to Scotus, Aquinas divides contingents into two
groups: those that either are, or essentially depend upon, the
actions of free agents, and those that are in no way connected
with free agents. In the first group there are actions like an
exhausted Socrates freely sitting down and the bursting of the
dam that Aristotle freely built. In the second group are such
actions as the earth moving around the sun and the rain falling
in Paris. Aquinas thinks that God wills the actions of the second group to be actual. He does this when he creates the uni-

verse and its laws, and he continues his willing activity by sustaining these laws. He thus can know these contingents through his willing activity.

On the other hand, God cannot, according to Aquinas, directly will the contingent actions of the first group to be actual. If he did, he would eliminate the freedom of the agents who perform them. At best, God can will to sustain the agents in their actions, but he cannot directly will them to perform the actions they perform. He cannot, consequently, know the actions of free agents through his own willing activity. He can know them only by their being present to his intellect.

Scotus, however, refuses to accept Aquinas' distinction between these two groups of contingents. According to Scotus, not only must God directly will the existence of the actions of agents who are not free, but he must also directly will the actions of free agents. Although Scotus did not specifically argue for this claim, I think we can explain his position in this way.

On Aquinas' position God knows the contingent acts of free agents because they are present to him in eternity. But these actions can be present to God only if the free agents themselves exist in time. And either these agents exist because God wills them to exist or they exist independently of God's will. Needless to say, Aquinas would hold the first alternative: The agents exist in time only because God wills them to exist. So on Aquinas' analysis, agents and their actions are present to God because God wills agents to exist in time.

From our point of view in time, this situation has the following consequence: Since God is omniscient, he knows all possibilities and knows what any possible person would do if created. When God creates an individual, he chooses to make actual one among all the possible persons he could create. This possible person is, in effect, an individual with a complete future (to us) history who, if created, will perform certain actions. So, in actualizing this person, God is making a person who will perform certain actions. He is, in effect, willing into existence not only the person, but also all the actions this person will perform.

Although this may appear surprising, it directly follows from God's omniscience. If God is omniscient, one must think that he would know which of the various possible persons he makes actual. But since possible persons are distinguished by their lifestories, this is equivalent to knowing which lifestory he brings into time. And the lifestory includes future (to us) actions.

So, if God knows which possible person he makes actual (as is required by his omniscience), he must will into existence both the person and the actions the person will perform.

This conclusion cuts against Aquinas' analysis of omniscience as understood by Scotus. Aquinas maintains that God knows the actions of actual free creatures through the presence of these actions to him in eternity. He makes this claim to avoid saying that God wills these actions to take place, for God's so willing is inconsistent with their freedom. Yet, given that God must create (from our point of view) individuals with complete, future histories in order for these actions to be present to his eternity, God must will both the individuals and their actions to exist. Thus, given God's omniscience, even the free actions of creatures must be willed to be actual by God, and consequently Aquinas cannot claim that God wills the actions of non-free agents to be actual but does not so will the actions of free agents.[30] His analysis of God's omniscience thus fails.

There seems, however, to be a serious and obvious problem with Scotus' general analysis of God's omniscience. According to his analysis, God determines which of those contingents not dependent upon free agents become actual by willing them to become actual. These contingencies are nevertheless contingent because God could will otherwise than he in fact does. The same analysis applies to the actions of free agents—particularly those of human beings. God determines what acts of free agents are actual, and these actions are contingent because God could will other actions than those he in fact wills. Nevertheless, these actions would not seem to be free since no free agent can act otherwise than God wills. Apparently, Scotus' analysis of omniscience rescues contingency, but it does so at the expense of the freedom of free agents—particularly human beings. His analysis seems incompatible with the freedom of free agents. In order to evaluate this apparent incompatibility, we must examine what Scotus means by 'freedom'. This is the subject of the next two chapters.

2 Scotus' Conception of Freedom: Libertarian Tendencies?

INTRODUCTION

Scotus is traditionally regarded as the champion of voluntarism. This attribution is justified, for he proposed scarcely a doctrine that was not in some way linked to his views on either the divine will or the wills of human beings. His discussions of the atonement and God's omniscience, for example, rest on his views about God's will; his analysis of how men come to have knowledge is connected with his views about the relationship of the intellect to the will. Given Scotus' emphasis on the will, it is surprising how little has been written on what Scotus means by 'freedom'.

If one were to canvass historians about Scotus' view of freedom, very likely one would find that most consider him a libertarian. And it is reasonable to suppose that anyone emphasizing the power and activity of the will as heartily as Scotus does would embrace a libertarian definition of 'freedom'. Perhaps this near unanimity about Scotus explains why so little work has been done on his understanding of freedom; it is, after all, pointless to enlarge upon the obvious.

Nonetheless, it is not at all evident, from an examination of Scotus' writings, just what he means by 'freedom'. Contrary to the common view, which labels him as a libertarian, Scotus states in many passages that determination is compatible with freedom of the will—a position in no way consistent with libertarianism. Such non-libertarian remarks stand side by side with other quite libertarian-sounding claims, so that the student of Scotus must wonder whether Scotus has any consistent view of freedom.

In spite of these difficulties, it can be shown that Scotus does have a consistent view of freedom. It is not, however, the libertarianism usually attributed to him. In order to clarify Scotus' conception of freedom, I shall examine in the present chapter a number of texts often regarded as presenting a libertarian view. By analyzing these texts as well as comments about them in the secondary literature, I shall show that Scotus is not, in fact, a libertarian. In the next chapter I shall explain in greater detail what Scotus' real understanding of freedom is.

ORDINATIO I, DISTINCTIONS 38 AND 39

Scotus discusses the nature of freedom in a number of his writings. Those scholars concerned with the issue usually focus on two principal texts: *Ordinatio,* Book I, distinctions 38 and 39, and the various versions of his commentary on the *Sentences,* Book II, distinction 25.[1] Although these two texts do stand out in importance for determining Scotus' view of freedom, it is useful to mention some of the other texts as well.

In discussing the enjoyment found in the beatific vision, Scotus claims that the human will can refrain from willing the perfect good (the beatific vision) because the will not only is able to will or not to will any good, but also has the freedom to act or not to act.[2] He also cites Augustine's remarks in his *Retractions* that "nothing is as much in the control of the will as the will itself" and comments that this saying should be understood as claiming that the will has control over the acts it causes.[3] In addition, he claims that the will does not will necessarily, and adds, in his discussion of whether an evil angel necessarily wills evil, that nothing other than the will determines the will to act.[4]

When Scotus discusses whether there are only two wills in Christ,[5] he claims that the will is the master of its own acts.[6] He further remarks that the will can elicit or not elicit acts that are and acts that are not in line with its inclinations.[7] He amplifies these ideas in his discussion of the moral virtues, where he says that the will determines itself[8] and that the will is free not only for opposite acts, but is free also in the way it acts.[9] Scotus makes similar remarks in the question "whether the resurrection is natural."[10]

Finally, in discussing whether all things desired are desired on account of beatitude,[11] Scotus distinguishes two desires of the will: a natural desire and a free desire. The natural desire is not a free power according to Scotus; it necessarily seeks beatitude. The free desire, on the other hand, is not determined to seek beatitude. As its name implies, it is a free power.

These scattered passages certainly present a strong picture of the will as free and unfettered by any external agent. They also seem to indicate that Scotus identifies freedom with the ability to perform an action and the ability to refrain from performing an action. This conclusion is reinforced by the text of *Ordinatio,* Book I, distinctions 38 and 39. As we have already seen, the majority of this text is devoted to presenting Scotus' analysis of God's omniscience. Nevertheless, a significant portion contains important remarks about freedom. Indeed, Scotus elsewhere refers to this section of his writings as containing solutions to important questions about freedom.[12]

Scotus claims in *Ordinatio* I, distinctions 38 and 39 that human wills have three different types of freedom:

> . . . I say that the will, insofar as it is first act, is free for opposite acts. It is also free, by means of those opposite acts, for the opposite objects to which it tends, and, further, for the opposite effects it produces.[13]

In commenting on these three freedoms, Scotus claims, in the first place, that the "freedom for opposite acts" is necessarily associated with the mutability of the will. This is so because this freedom is simply the ability to will something for a time and then to cease to will it. Obviously, in order for such a freedom to exist, the will must change. Scotus further points out that the second freedom (the ability to tend towards opposite objects) should not be confused with the third freedom (the ability to tend towards opposite effects), since one can tend towards an object without producing any effect.[14] Finally, Scotus claims that the second freedom is not necessarily connected with mutability. Some agent can will opposite objects without suffering any change in its will. (Scotus undoubtedly has in mind the divine will since, according to him, the divine will in one, eternal, immutable act wills all the diverse states of affairs in the universe; through the same act it therefore wills such opposite acts as Plato's sitting and Socrates' running.)[15] Having made these various distinctions, Scotus focuses on the first freedom—the ability to tend towards opposite acts.

Scotus claims that this freedom involves two powers. The first is what he calls an "evident power," and is the power for opposite acts in succession. Possessing this power, an agent has the ability to will an act (e.g., to swim in a pool) and then to cease to will the act (e.g., to cease to swim). These actions are, and must be, successive, for Scotus points out that it is nothing simultaneously to will and not will the same thing.[16]

The second power falling under the freedom for opposite acts is what Scotus calls a "not-so-evident power for opposites apart from any succession." He introduces this power in his attempt to solve a puzzle: How can a created will that exists for only one instant and wills something for that instant not will necessarily? The difficulty of the puzzle lies precisely in that this will exists for only an instant—the instant at which it wills. Since it does not exist prior to the instant, one cannot say that it wills freely by claiming that, prior to the time it willed, it had the ability to will otherwise. If the will in question is free, it must be free because of some feature obtaining at the instant at which it exists and wills.

Scotus claims in his solution to the puzzle that the will that exists for only an instant has (and, for that matter, all free wills have) a "not-so-evident power [for opposites] apart from any succession" at the instant at which it wills.[17] According to Scotus, this not-so-evident power is a real ability of the will of the agent to "posit its contingent effect in existence in such a way that, as naturally prior (to that act), it could equally well posit another opposite effect in existence."[18] Since the will has this ability, it is free during the instant of its existence.

As this not-so-evident power is difficult to understand, let us look at an example: At t_1 I hit a nail with a hammer. On Scotus' analysis, at t_1 I have the not-so-evident power not to hit the nail with the hammer at t_1. Scotus' claim here might strike us as odd. One might want to say that prior to t_1, since I am a free agent, I had both the ability to hit the nail and the ability not to hit the nail. When I hit the nail at t_1, however, it does not make sense to say that I retain the ability not to hit the nail at t_1. For if I have this ability at t_1, concurrent with hitting the nail, it seems as if I can simultaneously both hit the nail at t_1 and not hit the nail at t_1. Scotus explicitly rejects this construction of the not-so-evident power.[19] He acknowledges that opposite acts cannot exist simultaneously, viz., if I, in fact, hit the nail at t_1, I cannot also, in fact, not hit the nail at t_1. One or the other of two contradictories must be in fact true at any instant of time. How then can we understand the not-so-evident power Scotus thinks human wills possess?

Following Scotus, let us stipulate that at any instant of time t_n at which a will exists, we can talk about that will in a number of ways. We can, of course, talk about the will that exists at t_n as causing a certain act to be performed; Scotus calls this state of the will *qua* causing an act "the will in second act." We can also talk about the will existing at t_n as being in potentiality to causing an act and also as being in potentiality to not causing this act. Scotus calls this state of the will as being in potentiality to both acts "the will in first act." According to Scotus, the will in first act is naturally prior to the will in second act; that is, the will in second act is just a certain actualization of the will in first act, and thus the existence of the will in second act presupposes the existence of the will in first act.[20] Scotus also assumes that the order of natural priority can be analyzed by an order of "instants of nature," which are modeled on instants of time.[21] For example, a will in first act is said to exist at "instant of nature$_n$" (for short, n_n) and a will in second act is said to exist at "instant of nature$_{n+1}$" (n_{n+1}). Scotus also assumes that there can be many instants of nature at any one instant of time. Thus, at instant of time t_1 there may be instants of nature n_1, n_2, and so on. Given this mechanism, Scotus' not-so-evident power can be explained in this way: At t_1, when my will causes me to hit the nail, I can describe my will as being simultaneously in second act (causing the nail to be hit) and in first act (in potentiality to not causing the nail to be hit) as long as I think of these different descriptions as describing the will at different instants of nature. I can, therefore, talk about my will existing at both n_1 and n_2 at the same temporal time t_1. Because my will at t_1 can be said to exist at both n_1 and n_2, I can be said to cause contingently whatever I cause at t_1, for I could have done other than I, in fact, did at t_1.

In elaboration of this not-so-evident power, Scotus says it is a real power that has associated with it "a logical power, which is the compatibility of terms."[22] As part of his explanation of this logical power, Scotus introduces the distinction between the composed sense and divided sense of sentences. In the case of the will willing at a particular instant, the relevant sentence he discusses is: "The will, not willing something for t_1, can will it for t_1." If this sentence is understood in the composed sense, it is to be read as: "The will while not willing something for t_1 can will it for t_1." Here, the characterization of the will—'not willing something for t_1'—is combined with the noun, 'the will', to constitute the subject of the sentence. If the sentence is understood in the divided sense, it is to be read as: "The will, which is not willing something for t_1, can will it for t_1." Here, the characterization is divided from the noun, which is the simple subject of the sentence. According to Scotus, the sentence is false when taken in the composed sense, but true when taken in the divided sense:

> Taken in the sense of composition, viz., that there is a possibility that the will should simultaneously will [something] for t_1 and not will it for t_1, it is false. Taken in the sense of division, it is true. For then it signifies that the will of which "wills [something] for t_1" is truly asserted, could have "does not will it for t_1" truly asserted of it—but not in such a way that the latter and the former are simultaneously so asserted, but in such a way that when "does not will" is asserted, "wills" is not asserted.[23]

Scotus says that these different senses of the various sentences mark out a logical power of the will. He seems to think that the logical power is distinct from the not-so-evident power.

It is, however, difficult to understand what Scotus means by the logical power. We do not regard the "compatibility of terms" as a power; this seems to be just a mistake. But rather than saddle Scotus with apparent nonsense, perhaps we should think of what Scotus calls a "logical power" as his attempt to explain, through an analysis of sentences, what is involved in the not-so-evident power.[24]

In any event, Scotus acknowledges four objections to his analy-

sis of the not-so-evident power, and although Scotus' formulations and responses to the objections are intriguing, it will not
serve our purposes to focus on their complexities. It is sufficient,
I think, to note that, having met these objections, Scotus con-
siders himself justified in using the not-so-evident power to
explain the free action of a being that exists for only an instant.[25]

Scotus also uses the not-so-evident power to explain how
God freely and contingently wills what is external to his essence.
Scotus employs this device because he cannot explain how God
can will things freely and contingently by the "evident power for
opposites in succession." This evident power can be found only
where there is a succession of volitions in the free agent or
where the same volition can be successively directed to objects.
Since there can be no succession either of volitions or of acts in
God, who is simple and immutable, he cannot possess the evident
power. Hence, in the following passage, Scotus attributes to
God the not-so-evident power:

> For just as our will, as naturally prior to its act, elicits the
> act in such a way that it could, at the same instant [of
> time] elicit the opposite; so the divine will, insofar as it
> alone is naturally prior to its volition, tending to such an
> object does so contingently in such a way that at the same
> instant, i.e., the now of eternity, it could tend towards the
> opposite object.[26]

The passage can be explained in this way. In a certain instant of
nature, n_x, the divine will causes a certain act a to come to exist
in willed existence. This volition of the divine will is a free act
since, at a prior instant of nature, n_{x-1}, the divine will has both
the ability to cause a to come to exist in willed existence and the
ability to cause not-a to come to exist in willed existence. It is
thus free at a prior instant of nature, n_{x-1}, to posit at a later
instant of nature, n_x, the opposite of what it in fact posits at n_x.
This freedom is a major part of Scotus' claim that the divine will
wills contingently all that it wills external to itself.

Scotus' analysis of the not-so-evident power for opposites in
Ordinatio I, distinctions 38 and 39 is obviously complex and
challenging. In general, however, it appears that Scotus here
identifies freedom with the possession of this not-so-evident
power. Yet, in the texts we noted at the beginning of the chapter,
Scotus seemed to link freedom with the ability to perform an

action and the ability to refrain from performing the action. Does *Ordinatio* I, distinctions 38 and 39 mark a departure from this simpler view of freedom? I think not. On the contrary, his discussion of the not-so-evident power reinforces his linking of freedom with the ability to perform an action and the ability to refrain from performing an action. To see this, however, we must examine the assumptions Scotus makes in the text.

In *Ordinatio* I, distinctions 38 and 39, it is clear that Scotus equates the freedom of God and the freedom of free agents existing for only a temporal instant with the not-so-evident power for opposites. It is important to realize that both these types of agents are known with certainty to be free. God is, for Scotus, the most free of all agents. Similarly, in the puzzle about the will willing for one instant, Scotus assumes that the will is free. His task is to explain *how* such a will is free. Thus Scotus uses the not-so-evident power not to establish that these agents are free, but only to explain how it is that they are free. As we have seen, Scotus appealed to this power because neither of these types of agents exists for more than a single temporal instant. The will that wills for an instant exists for only one temporal instant; God, since he is timeless, exists altogether outside the succession of time.

The case of other temporal agents, and especially human agents, is very different. There is a real question as to whether these agents are free. Scotus does not assume that they are, nor can he reasonably appeal to a not-so-evident power for opposites to establish their freedom. Merely claiming that they have such a power does not prove their freedom. Scotus must first show that they in fact have the power before using it to indicate their freedom. It is interesting that Scotus' strategy for showing that ordinary agents have the not-so-evident power for opposites is to establish that they are free. He does this by determining whether the agent that exists for more than one temporal instant and performs an action at some instant can at the instant prior to his action refrain from performing the action. In this strategy, Scotus obviously assumes that if an agent has the relevant abilities it will also have the not-so-evident power for opposites.[27]

Thus, Scotus does not identify the freedom of temporal agents existing for more than one instant with the not-so-evident power for opposites. On the contrary, he regards the not-so-evident power as following from the freedom of this type of agent to cause or refrain from causing an action at a temporal instant prior to the temporal instant of the action. If such an agent is free in this sense, it will have the not-so-evident power. The reverse, however, is not true; it does not follow from the fact that an agent has the not-so-evident power that the agent is free to cause or refrain from causing an action at a temporal instant prior to the instant of the action. Agents existing for no more than one instant obviously lack the ability to cause or refrain from causing an action at a temporal instant prior to the action. Thus, Scotus' comments about the not-so-evident power seem to reinforce the view that Scotus equates the freedom of human agents (and of agents existing for more than one instant) with the ability to perform an action and the ability to refrain from performing the action. Let us now examine the second major text.

BOOK II, DISTINCTION 25 OF SCOTUS' COMMENTARIES ON THE *SENTENCES*

Medieval theologians, following the standard format, used their commentaries on the *Sentences* to discuss issues concerning free will. Since most schoolmen thought that the freedom of an agent rested upon the freedom of the agent's will, they usually discussed freedom by investigating whether the will itself or something external to it caused the will to act. Presumably, only if the will was the source of its own acts could it be considered free.

Following the tradition, in Book II, distinction 25 of his commentaries on the *Sentences,* Scotus treats the question "Whether anything other than the will causes effectively the act of willing." Several people have investigated Scotus' treatment. Balič has done much needed textual work.[28] Bonansea, in "Duns Scotus' Voluntarism," uses this section to illustrate the relationship between the intellect and the will in the writings of Scotus.[29] Finally, Lawrence Roberts, in *John Duns Scotus and the Concept of Human Freedom* and in his article of the same title, uses it to discuss general issues about Scotus' view on freedom.[30]

There are at least three major versions of the question. The Vivès-Wadding edition of Scotus' works presents a version that Scotus gave while at Paris, and that he later abandoned. Nevertheless, parts of the question are very similar to parts of the other two major versions of the question. The second version, found in Balič's *Les Commentaires de Jean Duns Scot sur les quatre livres de Sentences,* is from the *Additiones Magnae* of William of Alnwick. This work is a compilation of material from reports of Scotus' lectures at Paris and Oxford. Finally, we have a third version of the question presented by Balič in "Une question inédite de J. Duns Scot sur la Volonté." According to Balič, this version, given at Oxford, contains Scotus' final view. Following Balič and Roberts, I shall restrict most of my comments to the latter two versions of the question. Even though there are some differences between the two, the basic positions elaborated in them are so similar that the two texts can be discussed as offering essentially the same doctrine.

Both versions begin by presenting opinions to the effect that something other than the will is the effective cause of willing. Several views are put forth, including views attributed to Aristotle and Augustine. Having set forth these opinions, Scotus focuses on three specific positions.

The first position is that of Godfrey of Fontaines, who held, according to Scotus, that the phantasm is the principal cause determining the act of the will. Scotus rejects this view for two reasons. First, it regards the will as a non-voluntary agent. That is, on this view, the will could act only one way in relation to any phantasm. Second, this view is based on the mistaken metaphysical doctrine that mover and moved cannot be found simultaneously in the same subject.[31]

The second position is that of Aquinas, who claims, according to Scotus, that the moving cause of the will is the object known by the intellect. Scotus dismisses this position because it makes the will a non-voluntary agent that can only passively respond in predetermined ways to what the intellect presents to it.[32]

The third position Scotus treats is that of Henry of Ghent.[33] While both Godfrey and Aquinas seem to make the will a non-voluntary agent, Henry, by contrast, maintains that "Only the will is the efficient cause in regard to the act of willing, and the known object is only a *sine qua non*." Scotus opposes a variety of arguments to this position. Some of these arguments are directed against the whole notion of a *sine qua non* cause. Others are intended to reduce the position of Henry to absurdity. Still others are intended to show that the position makes ranking of various volitional objects impossible.[34]

Scotus' own position is that the intellect, the known object, and the will are all cooperating partial causes of volition. The will, however, is the principal agent of the three partial causes.[35]

In explaining this position, Scotus distinguishes three types of partial causation. The first type occurs when similar kinds of causes act together—though without influencing one another—to bring about a result. This type of partial causation occurs, for example, when two people pull a cart. The second type of partial causation occurs when one of the same kind of cooperating causes is subordinate to the other cause in the act of causing— for example, the motion of one stick that is moved by another stick that is in turn being moved by the hand of some agent. The third type occurs when one of the cooperating agents is a more important agent than the other(s). Scotus gives as an example the procreation of a child by a mother and father. (Given medieval views, the father, as contributor of the *form* of the child, is regarded as the more important agent in procreation.) Scotus classifies the relationship obtaining among the intellect, the known object, and the will as an example of this third type of causation.

It is clear from Scotus' explanation that he regards the will as a voluntary agent and as the principal source of its own actions. While the known object and the intellect may co-act with the will, they do not restrict the will so that it can act in only one way given a particular set of circumstances. Since Scotus thinks that the activities of the will are connected to the freedom of agents, we can use his remarks on the will as the effective cause of its own acts to help establish his understanding of freedom.

Lawrence Roberts, who has written extensively on the texts of Book II, distinction 25, spends considerable time arguing that these texts show that Scotus does not think that the actions of the will uniquely follow from the will's circumstances and prior conditions.[36] That is, he says Scotus denies that the will must act in the same way whenever the same circumstances and prior conditions obtain. Roberts demonstrates this quite successfully. He shows how Scotus repeatedly employs Augustine's argument in *The City of God*—which states that different men with the same dispositions and prior conditions act in different ways—to show that the actions of the will do not uniquely follow from the will's circumstances and prior conditions.[37] Roberts further shows how Scotus' belief that the will can act differently in the same circumstances is assumed in his arguments against the positions of Aquinas, Godfrey, and Henry on the effective cause of the will's activity.

Roberts is concerned to show that Scotus believes the will

capable of acting differently in the same circumstances in order
to argue that Scotus does not consider the will to be determined.
Establishing this is important for Roberts since he holds that
determinism is inconsistent with libertarianism, which is the
view he ascribes to Scotus.[38] Roberts is, of course, correct in
viewing determinism as incompatible with libertarianism. Scotus
does, however, allow that a human will can be both determined
and free. He consequently cannot endorse a libertarian definition of 'freedom'.

To understand why Scotus should not be labeled a libertarian,
we must first define 'libertarianism'. A number of definitions
have been given of this term, the least controversial of which is
this: An agent is free if and only if the agent has the ability and
opportunity to perform an action and the ability and opportunity to refrain from performing the action.[39] According to this
definition, an agent's ability to perform an action and to refrain
from performing the action is a necessary but not sufficient
condition for being libertarian-free relative to the action. In
addition, the agent must have the opportunity to exercise his
ability to perform the action and the opportunity to exercise his
ability to refrain from performing the action. If he lacks either
opportunity, he cannot be considered libertarian-free relative to
the action. As it turns out, Scotus' definition of 'freedom' fails
this latter condition and thus cannot be construed as a libertarian definition of 'freedom'.

We can see this by turning to this passage in distinction 25:

> My response to the question is, therefore, that nothing
> other than the will can be the total cause of volition in the
> will, but that the will freely determines itself to cause the
> act of willing. Which I prove in this way: Suppose that
> something occurs contingently in things so that at that
> instant at which it occurs it can fail to occur, so that it
> occurs avoidably; then I ask from what cause it occurs con-
> tingently: whether from a cause determined to one part of
> a contradiction or from a cause undetermined to either
> part. However, if from a cause that is determined in the
> first way, which is determined of itself to its occurrence,
> then it does not occur contingently and indeterminately
> or avoidably. Therefore, it occurs because of a cause which
> of itself is undetermined to either part. It is necessary
> that such a cause be determined to produce determinately;

therefore, it is determined either by itself or by something else. If by something else, then either it is necessarily determined by it and then it would necessarily produce the effect, that is, unavoidably, just as would happen if it were determined of itself to one part; *if it were contingently determined by the other, then it is in its own power to determine or not to determine;* it is not a natural cause—therefore it is the will. However, if it is determined by itself, then if it is necessarily determined, it would produce either opposites or nothing. However, if it determines itself contingently, that cause can be nothing but the will, because every other cause determines naturally.[40] [emphasis mine]

Scotus is explaining in this passage how human beings can perform free and contingent actions. According to Scotus, if there are free and contingent actions, there must be a free and contingent cause, i.e., a cause that is undetermined either to causing an action or to causing its contrary. Scotus identifies the free and contingent cause with the will and seems to claim here that the will determines itself. However, in the lines I have emphasized he allows the possibility that the will is determined and yet retains the ability to will an action and the ability to refrain from willing the action. Scotus allows this possibility because in the passage he distinguishes between an agent that is necessarily determined and an agent that is contingently determined by a cause. Both types of agents are determined, but they are determined in different ways. If an agent is necessarily determined by a cause, the agent acts necessarily because the action it produces is the only action it could produce. On the other hand, if an agent is only contingently determined by a cause, the agent acts contingently; according to Scotus, this means that the agent retains the ability to perform the action and the ability not to perform the action. Thus, a human will can have the ability to perform an action and the ability to refrain from performing the action and be determined by another agent so long as it is only contingently determined by the agent.

As I shall show in the next chapter, these distinctions between different forms of determination are motivated by Scotus' views about God's knowing and willing activities. For now it is important only to note that the passage is detrimental to establishing that Scotus holds a libertarian notion of freedom, for it shows that Scotus thinks that the will can somehow be determined yet free. And determinism is incompatible with libertarianism. As the passage also shows, the ability of an agent to act differently in similar circumstances does not show that the agent is free in a libertarian sense. According to Scotus, an agent can act differently in similar circumstances if it is contingently determined by an agent that itself wills contingently.

With these lessons in mind, let us briefly return to the texts examined at the beginning of the chapter. As is the case for *Ordinatio* I, distinctions 38 and 39, and the various versions of Book II, distinction 25, Scotus talks in these texts only about the abilities of agents (or the wills of agents). He affirms throughout that a free agent is able to will or not will any good, and that, in addition, it can refrain from acting according to its inclinations since it does not act necessarily. But, as we have seen, these affirmations do not entail a libertarian definition of 'freedom'. In order to advance such a definition, Scotus would need to show that free agents have the opportunities to exercise these abilities. He does not, however, attempt this. As we shall see in the next chapter, there are reasons that Scotus does not.

3 Scotus' Conception of Freedom: His Non-Libertarian View

OPUS OXONIENSIS IV, DISTINCTION 49,
  QUESTION 6

Those who regard Scotus as a libertarian must suffer surprise when they examine his comments in *Opus Oxoniensis* IV, distinction 49, question 6.[1] His remarks in this text are scarcely consistent with a libertarian view of freedom.

This section of Scotus' commentary on the *Sentences* concerns the question, "whether permanence pertains to the beatific vision," and in particular whether the blessed are free to refrain from enjoying the vision. Scotus is, of course, working out of a tradition that holds that the blessed in heaven do enjoy the beatific vision, but this tradition is not specific about whether the blessed can refrain from enjoying it. Thomas Aquinas, Godfrey of Fontaines, and Henry of Ghent all affirm that the blessed are necessitated in their enjoyment and cannot refrain from enjoying the vision.[2] The three men express this by saying that the blessed are "impeccable" as regards their enjoyment.

Scotus agrees that the blessed are impeccable. He cautions, however, that one must be clear about the meaning of this word.

According to Scotus, the sentence "the blessed are impeccable" can be understood in either a composed or a divided sense. Read in the composed sense, the sentence states that the blessed cannot refrain from the beatific vision and still be blessed. This is so because it is part of the meaning of 'blessed' that the person who is blessed enjoys the vision. If those who say that the blessed are impeccable mean this in a composed sense, Scotus has no disagreement with them.

The sentence read in the divided sense can be understood in two different ways. Read in the first way, it states that the person who is blessed lacks the intrinsic ability to refrain from enjoying the beatific vision. Read in the second way, it states that the person who is blessed has the intrinsic ability to refrain from the vision but does not refrain because of some external factor. Scotus rejects the first reading of the divided sense because it entails that the blessed cannot refrain from the vision and thus are not free in their enjoyment of it. The second reading, which he accepts, safeguards the freedom of the blessed. Thus Scotus agrees verbally with his predecessors in stating that the blessed are impeccable as regards their enjoyment of the beatific vision. In spirit, however, Scotus disagrees with them by claiming that the blessed have the ability to refrain from the enjoyment.

Even though Scotus affirms that the blessed have this ability, he claims that they will never exercise it, and that, consequently, their enjoyment of the vision is perpetual. He attributes this guarantee to God's activity: God ensures that the blessed will never exercise their ability to refrain from the vision by blocking any attempt to exercise it. Thus, it is God who guarantees the perpetuity of the enjoyment of the beatific vision rather than some intrinsic power of the blessed since, intrinsically, the blessed are able to refrain from the vision.

In answering whether the beatific vision of the blessed is perpetual, Scotus thus balances two claims. On the one hand, he wants to affirm that the blessed are free in their enjoyment of the vision. He therefore affirms that they have the ability to refrain from the vision. On the other hand, he also affirms that the vision is perpetual. He argues for this by claiming that God ensures that the blessed will not exercise their ability to refrain from the vision.

It appears, then, that in this question Scotus identifies freedom with the ability to perform an action and the ability to refrain from performing the action. Whether these abilities are exercised does not enter into determining an agent's freedom. As long as the agent possesses the abilities—even if they will not be exercised—the agent is free. According to Scotus, since the blessed have both the ability to enjoy the beatific vision and the ability to refrain from enjoying the vision, they are free in their enjoyment of the vision.[3]

Many objections to Scotus' position immediately arise, the most obvious of which is whether the blessed do indeed have the ability to refrain from enjoying the beatific vision. If they never will refrain from the vision, since God will prevent them from exercising their ability to refrain, can one say that they have the ability? Put more generally, one can ask whether an ability that will not be exercised is really an ability.

Scotus, in fact, presents this very objection to his argument:

> Moreover, it will not be in the power of the will to act thus or not act thus because [when] something is determined by a superior agent, it is not in the power of the determined to act thus or not act thus; for it acts as moved by the determining agent. Therefore, this act will not be praiseworthy or even, properly speaking, voluntary.[4]

This passage poses the objection very clearly: If an agent determines another agent not to perform an action, does the determined agent have the ability to perform the action? In the case at hand, God determines the blessed never to refrain from the beatific vision, and they will therefore never refrain from the vision. Consequently, according to the objection, they do not have the ability to refrain from the vision and thus are not free in their enjoyment of it.

Scotus' reply is very provocative. He claims that determination of an agent by an agent that is metaphysically superior to the agent does not infringe on the freedom of the lower agent. Only determination by an agent that is metaphysically inferior to the agent in question is contrary to the freedom of this agent.[5] Although Scotus does not here spell out just what he means by 'metaphysically superior' or 'metaphysically inferior', he does so to a large extent in his *De Primo Principio* where he discusses the various essential orders of causation. For present purposes, we need only point out that God is considered by all medieval thinkers to be metaphysically superior to every other being.

Moreover, agents like the sun, rocks, plants, and non-human animals are regarded as metaphysically inferior to men.

In any event, Scotus provides reasons for making the distinction between determination by metaphysically inferior agents and determination by superior agents. According to Scotus, part of what is meant by a metaphysically superior agent is that it is powerful enough to prevent the actions of agents inferior to it. Thus, a metaphysically superior agent can determine the activity of an inferior agent by controlling the actions of the inferior agent. But on the other hand, a metaphysically inferior agent can determine a metaphysically superior agent only indirectly, by affecting the nature of the superior agent so that it acts in a certain way. It can determine only in this way because, by definition, it cannot prevent the actions of superior agents.

Scotus' point here is not completely idiosyncratic. In the Christian tradition, it is held that God can prevent the actions of created agents. Thus many people complain when God does not prevent a madman from harming innocent people by rendering the madman's actions ineffective. Moreover, believers in astrology hold that the stars influence our natures such that we are of certain characters or act in certain ways. They hold this while simultaneously believing that the stars cannot by their direct intervention prevent actions or render actions ineffective.

Scotus' distinction between the two types of determination does help to answer the objection posed above. If we accept the distinction, we can draw these conclusions: A metaphysically inferior agent determines a superior agent only by causing internal constraints in the nature of the superior agent. A metaphysically superior agent, however, determines an inferior agent by controlling the actions of the inferior agent and not by constraining the nature of the inferior agent.[6] For Scotus, the abilities of agents to act in one way or another derive from the nature of agents. They thus are internal abilities and would be affected by internal constraints. Actions follow these abilities, but the presence or absence of actions is not to be confused with the presence or absence of abilities. Thus, a metaphysically superior agent can determine an inferior agent without affecting the abilities of the agent; it will affect only the actions of the agent. A metaphysically inferior agent, on the other hand, can determine superior agents only by affecting their abilities. It follows from Scotus' remarks that God can determine the blessed's enjoyment of the beatific vision without affecting their ability to refrain from the vision. Of course, Scotus can conclude from this that the blessed are free in their enjoyment of the vision only if he identifies freedom with the possession of the ability to perform an action and the ability to refrain from the action. Scotus, as we have seen, is very willing to accept this link. It is on this basis that he maintains that the blessed are free in their enjoyment even though God guarantees that they will not refrain from the enjoyment.

There are, of course, a number of objections that can be offered against Scotus' argument. One of the most serious is an epistemological problem: How can we claim that an agent has an ability when he never exercises the ability? Typically, we say that an agent has an ability because we have seen him perform the relevant action. In the present case, however, we are not given this opportunity; the blessed never exercise the ability. Of course, in more ordinary cases we demonstrate that an agent has the ability to perform a certain action he never performs by showing that an agent has performed similar types of actions. For example, if we wonder whether an agent has the ability to see a rock on a table that is currently invisible due to optical tricks, we would point out that the agent has perceived other rocks. Since he has seen rocks before, we would assume that he has the ability to see the rock on the table. He cannot see it currently, even though he has the ability to see it, because his exercise of the ability is being impeded by the optical tricks.[7] But while this appeal to similar cases is convincing in ordinary situations, it is not convincing in the case of the blessed's vision. Quite simply, there is nothing sufficiently similar to the beatific vision to count as a parallel case for establishing abilities.

One can also object to Scotus' argument by questioning Scotus' belief that the blessed are free because they possess the ability to enjoy the vision and the ability to refrain from the enjoyment. People urging this objection would point out that there is more to freedom than the possession of abilities: The agent in question must also have the opportunity to exercise these abilities.[8] This distinction can be seen in this example. I have the ability to swim in the pool at my local YMCA since I can swim and am a member. Unfortunately, every Thursday night is "Seniors' Night" and only people over the age of sixty-five can use the pool that night. Since I am under sixty-five, the rule eliminates my opportunity on Thursday to exercise my ability to swim in the pool. Similarly, in the case of the beatific vision, the blessed perhaps have the ability to refrain from the vision, but they do not have the opportunity to exercise this ability since God would prevent the exercise. Thus, the blessed are not free.

This would be a good objection if Scotus accepted the definition of 'freedom' implicit in this objection: Freedom is the ability and opportunity to perform an action and the ability and opportunity to refrain from performing the action. (As I have indicated, I identify this notion of freedom with libertarianism.) Scotus does not, however, accept this libertarian notion of freedom, and the fact that this objection based on a libertarian notion can be raised against his analysis shows that Scotus does not endorse this view.

There is, however, a related objection. We might be willing to connect freedom with the ability to perform an action and the ability to refrain from performing the action as Scotus apparently does; but we would hardly want to identify them. If we did, then cases in which we would intuitively say that agents are not free would have to be thought of as cases in which agents are free. For example, if we identify the two, a human being who has the ability to rob from a poor box and the ability to refrain from robbing from the poor box but is forced at knifepoint to rob from a poor box would perform the action freely. The threat of violence does not, after all, compromise the agent's abilities; it only compromises what the agent does. Yet, Scotus does seem to identify freedom with the ability to perform an action and the ability to refrain from performing the action, and so it appears that he must agree to such counter-intuitive conclusions.

These objections do pose serious problems for Scotus' discussion in *Ordinatio* IV, distinction 49, question 6, and render his position implausible. Nevertheless, his discussion does underline two very basic assumptions Scotus makes about freedom. First of all, it is clear that Scotus distinguishes abilities from the exercise of abilities. While he allows that we usually mark out abilities through the exercise of relevant actions, possession of abilities is not to be identified with the performance of actions. Secondly, Scotus links freedom with the possession of both the ability to perform an action and the ability to refrain from the action. As we have seen, this is very different from a libertarian notion of freedom, and, consequently, Scotus does not offer such a notion of freedom. In order to clarify further the position Scotus is presenting, we need to turn to some other texts.

THE *QUODLIBETAL QUESTIONS*

Scotus' most direct and extensive discussion of the relationship between God's will and the free will of human beings is found in the *Quodlibetal Questions*, numbers 16 and 18.[9] Number 16—devoted to the question, "Are freedom of will and natural necessity compatible as regards the same act and object?"—is the more important of the two. Saint Augustine's writings play a key role in this question; in fact, Scotus opens the question by citing two texts from Augustine. He cites the first, which links culpability with voluntariness, to show that natural necessity and freedom of the will are not compatible.[10] The second citation, which points out that God is free even though he must know and will, states that natural necessity is not opposed to freedom.[11]

After citing Augustine and discussing whether there is necessity in any act of the will, Scotus makes a very important distinction. He distinguishes between the necessity of immutability and the necessity of inevitability. The necessity of immutability "excludes a change in will in which at some subsequent moment the divine will would will differently than at present."[12] That is to say, once the divine will wills something, it is not possible that the divine will not will it. The necessity of inevitability "not only excludes change or succession but rules out that the divine will could have willed other than it has."[13] That is, whatever the divine will wills, it had to will, and could not have willed otherwise. Obviously, the necessity of inevitability is much stronger than the necessity of immutability, and Scotus says that we can attribute the necessity of immutability but not the necessity of inevitability to God since doing so would make God unable to perform any action contingently. Even though Scotus distinguishes the two necessities in relation to the divine will, it is clear that he thinks the distinctions are also applicable to human wills.

Having made the distinction, Scotus claims:

> Although the divine will necessarily takes complacency in everything intelligible insofar as some participation of God's own goodness is revealed therein, it does not will necessarily any created thing with a volition that is efficacious or that determines it to exist. On the contrary, it wills the creature's existence contingently just as it causes it contingently. For if it necessarily willed it to be in this

second sense of necessity, it would cause it necessarily
with a necessity of inevitability, at least at that moment
when God wants it to exist.[14]

In this passage, Scotus assumes that the divine will does determine human wills, but that they are only contingently determined by the divine will. We have encountered contingent
causation before when we examined the texts of Scotus' commentaries on Book II, distinction 25, of the *Sentences*.[15] In those
texts, Scotus calls it "contingent determination" and seems to
mean this: When a human will wills something, it can either
will it necessarily or contingently. It wills something necessarily if it is not logically possible that it will something else, and it
wills contingently if it is logically possible that it will otherwise.
The divine will necessarily determines (or causes) a human will
whenever it determines the human will to will necessarily. Whenever the divine will determines the human will to will contingently, the divine will contingently determines the will. Clearly,
both contingent and necessary determination are forms of determination in the sense that God determines the human will to
will as it does. Nevertheless, if God only contingently determines the will to act in a certain way, the action of the agent is
contingent. It is still logically possible for the human will to will
something else; God merely needs to will it to will otherwise
and it will so will. Clearly, on this scheme, the contingent
volition of a human will depends upon God's contingent volition.
Indeed, Scotus is aware of this, and this is why he says in the
above passage that God does not act with a necessity of inevitability as regards human wills. If he were to act with this necessity,
he could only necessarily determine human wills.

The passage cited above is startling. If we are concerned
about the determination of a human will through God's will, it
would seem that it scarcely matters whether God contingently
or necessarily determines an agent. What matters is whether
the human will can act other than God wills it to act. If it can, it
would be undetermined. If it cannot, it would be determined
and, consequently, not free—unless Scotus held that freedom is
equivalent to contingency, i.e., an agent is free as regards x if
and only if the agent contingently wills x. Surprisingly, there are
several passages in which Scotus seems to affirm this equivalence.
For example, in the *Quodlibetal Questions,* number 18, Scotus
remarks:

... what all these have in common is that the acts to which they refer are in the free power of the agent. Now although this power involves both intellect and will, it is only the will, I say, that can completely account for the indifference or indeterminacy as regards the alternative—the indifference, namely, that consists in the fact that the action which occurred might not have occurred, or vice versa ["indifference to the alternative" must be understood here disjunctively, not conjunctively, that is to say, in *sensu divisio,* not in *sensu composito*].[16]

Here, Scotus links freedom with the possibility of an alternative. In two of the texts of his commentaries on the *Sentences,* Book II, distinction 25, Scotus says that whatever occurs contingently occurs avoidably.[17] Since Scotus thinks that if we perform an avoidable action we perform it freely, these texts are tantamount to an identification of freedom with contingency. Moreover, in *De Primo Principio* Scotus says that since the first cause causes contingently, it causes voluntarily.[18] Since Scotus identifies what is done voluntarily with what lies in the power of the will rather than with what is simply willed by the will, this passage also identifies contingency with freedom.[19]

Even though there are a number of passages in which Scotus seems to identify freedom with contingency, I think it would be a mistake to saddle Scotus with this claim.[20] Scotus' analysis of the relationship between God's volitions and the freedom of human agents is much more subtle. To see the subtlety, let us return to the *Quodlibetal Questions,* number 16.

Towards the end of the question Scotus remarks:

Every natural agent either is first in an absolute sense, or if not, it will be naturally determined to act by some prior agent. Now the will can never be an agent that is first in an absolute sense. But neither can it be naturally determined by a higher agent, for it is active in such a way that it determines itself to action in the sense that if the will wills something necessarily, for example A, this volition of A would not be caused naturally by that which causes the will even if the will itself were caused naturally, but once the first act by which the will is caused be given, if the will were left to itself and could have or not have this volition contingently, it would still determine itself to this volition.[21]

This passage is intriguing, for it suggests the following view: When a higher agent, e.g., God, determines the will to act, it accomplishes the determination through the will's own nature. That is, the higher agent determines the will to act in the way the will would act according to its nature even if it were not determined by the higher agent. On this view, the higher agent does not compel the will; on the contrary, it causes the will to act as it would choose to act. Indeed, Scotus reinforces this understanding when he says a few lines later:

> But if the caused will necessarily wills anything, it is not determined by its cause to will such in the way the weight is determined to descend. All it receives from the cause is a principle by which it determines itself to this volition.[22]

Again, in this passage, Scotus emphasizes that the higher agent determines the will by determining the will to act according to its nature. Moreover, this theme is also found in texts other than the *Quodlibetal Questions*. For example, in *Ordinatio* I, distinction 41, question unica, in discussing predestination, Scotus claims that God knows who will be damned because he sees himself cooperating with the damned in the sins of omission and commission leading to damnation.[23] God does not cause the sinner to sin. He merely allows the sinner to perform his sins and cooperates with these actions. The same point is echoed in *Ordinatio* I, distinction 47, question unica, in which Scotus discusses the nature of divine permission for actions.[24] These passages indicate that Scotus sees the divine will as determining the wills of human beings by cooperating with their volitions.

The view Scotus is presenting is in line with other parts of his philosophical system. In his analysis of God's omniscience, Scotus claims that God chooses which possible states of affairs are actual. Among the possibilities he has to choose from are: "Jeff Stout writes about ethics on his fellowship"; "Jeff Stout breaks the Olympic record in the 1500 meter freestyle on his fellowship"; and so on. The possibilities about Jeff Stout that God chooses to actualize constitute the individual Jeff Stout. So, in a sense, God does determine what Jeff Stout is by determining the nature that is the actual Jeff Stout, which is just the actualized composite of all his possible actions. God, of course, cooperates with the actions of Jeff Stout since he wants to cooperate with what he wills to be actual. God does not force Jeff Stout to do what he does. On the contrary, God ensures that Jeff Stout fulfills what his nature causes him to do.

This is the solution Scotus proposes in the *Quodlibetal Questions* to the problem of the determination of human wills through God's will. God does not determine a human will in the sense that he forces the will to act in a certain way. He merely wills the human will to act according to its nature. When the human will acts according to its nature, it is free.

Thus in passages about the relationship between God's will and the free actions of human beings, Scotus relies heavily on claims about what the will would choose of its own nature. This emphasis on what the will chooses in accordance with its nature is an element in Scotus' analysis of freedom we have not seen before. Nevertheless, it is a very important element because, as I have argued, determination through God's willing activity is an important issue for Scotus. Thus any final statement of Scotus' notion of freedom must take into account what the will would will according to its nature.

Although there are difficulties with Scotus' analysis of the relationship between God's willing activity and the free actions of men, I shall not address them now, but shall do so in later chapters. At the present time, I want to draw together the points of the preceding pages and present what I take to be Scotus' notion of freedom.

SCOTUS' CONCEPTION OF FREEDOM

From the preceding analysis of texts in this chapter and the last, it is obvious that Scotus does not have a simple view about freedom. In fact, he seems to endorse different views. Despite this appearance of inconsistency, I think he does propose a consistent view. For Scotus, an agent is free relative to an action only if the agent has the ability to perform the action and the ability to refrain from performing the action. The emphasis here is on ability. Scotus, as we have seen, does not identify abilities with their exercise. In fact, he would allow that there might be an ability to perform some action even if the agent would never perform the action.

Although Scotus does not identify abilities with their exercise, he does distinguish abilities through their exercise. For example, we know that Peter has the ability to see a rock on the table—even though he cannot now see it due to optical tricks—because he has in the past seen rocks. Thus, because an agent has exercised an ability in certain situations, we claim that in similar situations he has the ability. For Scotus, the fact that, for example, a man at a certain time decides to sin by stealing from the poor box and at another time, in similar situations, decides not to steal proves that the man has the ability to steal and the ability not to steal from the poor box. He is consequently free to steal (and free not to steal).

If we can judge from Scotus' remarks about the not-so-evident power for opposites (discussed in the previous chapter), it appears that Scotus thinks that the ability to steal and the ability not to steal obtain immediately before an action for agents who exist for more than one temporal instant. That is, at the time immediately before my theft from the poor box (call it t_0) I have the ability to steal and the ability not to steal from the box. At the time of the action, I actualize one or the other possibility by stealing or refraining from stealing. (As we have seen, Scotus also thinks we retain the abilities at the time of the action t_1, and he appeals to instants of nature to explain this.) Scotus is justified in making this assumption since he distinguishes abilities from their exercise. When Scotus says that someone can do a certain action, he merely means that the person has the ability to perform the action. He does not mean that the person will in fact perform the action if he wants to. He might, for example, be prevented from carrying out the action by some external force.

A libertarian would, of course, dispute with Scotus at this point. The libertarian would say that mere ability is not enough to make an action free. In addition, one must have the opportunity to exercise the ability if one so desires. Thus, if someone has an ability but cannot exercise it, we would not say he is free. It is obvious, therefore, that Scotus does not advocate a libertarian notion of freedom since he does not require that there be the needed opportunities.

Yet, Scotus was aware, I think, that freedom was more than the possession of abilities. This was part of his motivation for claiming that an agent is free relative to God's activity not only by having abilities to perform and to refrain from performing, but also by acting in accordance with what it would will according to its nature. If the agent were in some sense forced against its nature by God's activity, the agent would not be free, even though it possessed the ability to perform an action and ability to refrain from the action.[25] Moreover, although Scotus does not explicitly state this, it seems reasonable to extend this point to cover all cases in which the actions of other agents compromise the activities of human agents. Whenever an agent's actions are prevented or caused by another agent, the agent freely performs its actions only if the actions it performs are those it would will according to its nature. Indeed, at least one remark Scotus makes confirms this view:

> Something may well be necessary in itself with a necessity repugnant to freedom and still be accepted freely and contingently. For instance, if one voluntarily dives off a cliff and, while falling, continues to will this, he falls necessarily with the necessity of natural gravity and yet he freely wills that fall.[26]

This passage indicates that Scotus thinks that a human agent's actions may be both necessitated and free as long as the agent wishes the actions.

In summary, Scotus presents a complex view of freedom. In fact, it is a two-part view: An agent is free as regards action x if and only if (1) the agent has the ability to perform x and the ability to refrain from performing x, and (2) the agent wills the performance (or the refraining from the performance) of x in accordance with his nature.

SCOTUS ON OMNISCIENCE AND FREEDOM

Given Scotus' two-part definition of freedom, the apparent conflict between his analysis of God's omniscience and the ability of men to perform free actions seems to dissolve. God knows what occurs because he directly wills into existence all actual events. He does this by willing certain possible events not connected with any free agent to become actual as well as by willing into existence certain possible persons. As we have seen, these possible persons are collections of possible properties and so, when God wills the possible persons to be actual, he is willing into existence persons who perform certain actions.

God does not construct these possible persons. In a sense, the possible persons come ready-made to God, for he knows them as he knows all possibilities, through his intellect (which is a natural agent). God decides only which of the possible persons are to be actual. He thus allows certain persons to become actual who fulfill their natures and therefore satisfy the second part of the two-part definition of 'freedom'.

Scotus thinks that God's willing activity is not in conflict with the abilities of free agents to perform free actions and to refrain from performing the free actions. This is so because God contingently determines free agents; that is, for any action a free agent performs, God could have willed the agent to perform another action than the one he, in fact, performs. Moreover, since Scotus claims, as an empirical fact, that agents perform different actions under similar circumstances, he holds that free agents have the ability to perform free actions as well as the ability to refrain from performing free actions. Thus free agents fulfill the first part of his definition of 'freedom', and God's willing activity does not compromise their freedom.

There are, of course, a number of questions and criticisms that can be raised about Scotus' claims, and especially about the second clause of his definition of freedom. Although I want to raise and address these problems, I shall do this by examining the doctrines of some of Scotus' intellectual descendants. As we shall see, investigating the positions of such figures in the voluntarist tradition as Molina and Leibniz will highlight Scotus' views on God's omniscience in a most effective manner.

Part II
Scotus' Intellectual Descendants

4 Molina on God's Knowledge of Future Contingents

INTRODUCTION

Discussion of God's knowledge of future contingents and the ability of men to perform free actions did not, of course, cease after Scotus. In fact, the issue became a major source of controversy among the followers of Scotus at both Oxford and Paris. Ockham, for example, criticized Scotus' view of God's knowledge of future contingents and gave his own fideistic analysis.[1] Robert Holcot also relegated the problem of God's knowledge of future contingents to the realm of faith, while Jean Buridan analyzed the problem through a three-value logic. Thomas of Buckingham adopted certain Pelagian views in his attempt to deal with the problem, and Gregory of Rimini, as well as Pierre d'Ailly, criticized various proposed solutions. These issues were not, of course, the property of the scholastics alone, but were in fact the major interests of the two chief leaders of the Protestant Reformation, Martin Luther and Jean Calvin.

Luther's most systematic treatment of the problems surrounding God's knowledge of future contingents is his *De Servo Arbitrio* (*On the Enslaved Will*).[2] This work, published in 1525, was in response to Erasmus' work of 1524 entitled *Diatribe seu collatio de libero arbitrio* (*Discussion, or Collation, Concerning Free Will*), attacking Luther's views on free will.[3] Although the bulk of these two works concerns the interpretation of scriptural texts about free will, some sections are of philosophical interest.

Erasmus identifies God's foreknowledge with his willing activity but, by appealing to the distinction between the necessity of the inference and the necessity of the consequent, he argues that it does not conflict with the free action of men.[4] Given that the actions of men are necessary only by the necessity of the inference, they can do other than they do and, hence, according to Erasmus, are free. Luther rejects Erasmus' argument because of his own understanding of contingency and his claims about God's will. According to Luther, something is contingent only if it is done by a contingent and mutable will.[5] But God's will is not changeable according to Luther. On the contrary, it is governed by what Scotus called the "necessity of inevitability": the necessity that not only excludes change or succession, but also rules out that the divine will could have willed other than it has.[6] Since everything occurs through God's willing activity, it follows, according to Luther, that all events in the world are necessary.

Luther was, of course, aware that this claim seemed in conflict with free will. Yet, Luther claimed that freedom was not compromised since freedom is to be equated with the liberty of spontaneity (the agent in question acts in accordance with its wishes without external compulsion) and not with the liberty of indifference (the power to perform an action and the power to refrain from the action).[7] Thus, even though the actions of agents may be necessitated by God, they are free so long as the agents willingly perform the actions.

To Erasmus' credit, he understood Luther's position and attacked it for its absurd consequences.[8] Given Luther's scheme God seems extremely unjust. He wills men to sin, and, even though they have no choice about these actions, punishes them. Luther saw Erasmus' point as a major objection to his theory, and answered it by appealing to a contrast between the "light of glory" and the "lights of nature and grace":

> By the light of nature, it is inexplicable that it should be just for the good to be afflicted and the bad to prosper; but the light of grace explains it. By the light of grace, it is inexplicable how God can damn him who by his own

strength can do nothing but sin and become guilty. Both the light of nature and the light of grace here insist that the fault lies not in the wretchedness of man, but in the injustice of God; nor can they judge otherwise of a God who crowns the ungodly freely, without merit, and does not crown, but damns another, who is perhaps less, and certainly not more, ungodly. But the light of glory insists otherwise, and will one day reveal God, to whom alone belongs a judgment whose justice is incomprehensible, as a God Whose justice is most righteous and evident— provided only that in the meantime we *believe* it, as we are instructed and encouraged to do so by the example of the light of grace explaining what was a puzzle of the same order to the light of nature.[9]

This response is perhaps unconvincing to those less theologically oriented than Luther. Nonetheless, the appeal to faith is Luther's reply to what seems to be one of the most serious criticisms of a position endorsing a non-libertarian view of freedom.

Calvin's treatment of the problem of God's knowledge of future contingents is found in his *Institutes of the Christian Religion,* Book I, chapter fifteen, to Book II, chapter five.[10] Like Luther, Calvin in this 1536 work was primarily concerned with scriptural evidence for free will, but he commented on more philosophical issues as well. He indicated his familiarity with the medieval distinction between the necessity of the inference and the necessity of the consequent,[11] and he knew Lombard's views about the difference between freedom from compulsion and freedom from necessity.[12] Calvin claims to follow Augustine's view that freedom is to be identified with the liberty of spontaneity, and in fact he goes so far as to advocate eliminating the term 'free will', which is so closely tied to the libertarian view of freedom.[13] In general, then, Calvin's analysis of God's knowledge of future contingents is similar to Luther's, and against the criticism stating that his analysis makes God seem unjust, Calvin also appeals to faith in the teachings of scripture.[14]

In response to the Protestant Reformation, the Roman Catholic Church during the sixteenth century fostered what has been called the "Counter Reformation." This movement attempted to combat doctrines and to strengthen the position of the Church. Near the end of the century, a major controversy broke out between the Jesuits and the Dominicans concerning God's knowledge of future contingents. This controversy had several roots. The theologians of the Counter Reformation, interested in defeating the Protestant Reformers, attacked any view resembling Protestant doctrine. When the Jesuits, led by Luis de Molina, understood the Dominicans to be endorsing Protestant views on freedom, they condemned them. Undoubtedly, the traditional rivalry between the Dominicans and the Jesuits had much to do with this controversy, and differing interpretations of both Scotus' and Aquinas' views on omniscience added to the dispute as well.

In the present chapter, I shall examine the work of the major figure in the dispute, Luis de Molina. Not only did Molina analyze and criticize both Scotus' and Aquinas' work, but he also proposed his own solution to the problem of God's knowledge of future contingents: his doctrine of middle knowledge. Although Molina's doctrine is unsuccessful, examining it, together with his remarks about both Scotus and Aquinas, will reveal important aspects of the relationship between God's knowledge and human freedom; it will also highlight certain facets of Scotus' views on these issues.

MOLINA ON SCOTUS AND AQUINAS

Molina's major contributions to the discussion of God's knowledge of future contingents are his *Concordia Liberii Arbitrii cum Gratiae Donis, Divina Praescientia, Praedestinatione et Reprobantione* and his *De Scientia Dei*.[15] Both works are very complex because Molina attempts to do several things in them. He tries, first of all, to solve the problem of God's knowledge of future contingents, and, in addition, he examines both Aquinas' and Scotus' theories on the problem of future contingents. This last discussion is an intricate weaving of criticism and defense of the views of the two men. In order to sort out its complexities, it is best to begin by recounting briefly Molina's own theory.

According to Molina, it is necessary to posit three different types of knowledge in God:

> One [type] merely natural, which consequently can in no way be otherwise in God, through which he knows all that the divine power extends to either immediately or through the intervention of secondary causes. [He knows]

both the natures of singulars and the necessary relationships of them as well as contingents. [He does] not [know]
them as being in the future or as being determinately, but
[he knows them] as being able to be and not be, which is a
necessary feature of them, and thus falls under the natural
knowledge of God.

Another [type] simply free, by which God, after the free
act of his will and without any condition or hypothetical,
knows absolutely and determinately which from the collection of all possibilities are to be future and which are not.

Finally, the third [type is] middle knowledge by which
from the most elevated and inscrutable comprehension of
each free will in its essence it is understood what the free
will would do from its own natural freedom if it were
placed in this or that or any of the infinite number of
orders of things—even though it [the free will] could, if it
willed, do something opposite. . . . [16]

As we have seen, Scotus talks about the first type of knowledge
as God's knowledge of all that is logically possible, and he
describes the second type as those states of affairs God chooses
to make actual. Aquinas, too, says that God knows all possibles,
and he says that God knows what actually occurs through his
"knowledge of vision." Molina thinks, however, that these two
types of knowledge are insufficient to explain God's knowledge
of future contingents. He therefore claims that God has the
third type, middle knowledge. Through this type of knowledge,
God knows what every free agent would freely choose to do in
any circumstances whatsoever.

Molina defends his claim that God has this power by an
appeal to scripture—in particular the story of Chorazin and
Betsaida.[17] According to the story, Christ said to the citizens
of Chorazin and Betsaida—people evidently not interested in
Christ's message—that, had the miracles and other great works
that occurred at Chorazin and Betsaida been performed in Tyre
and Sidon, the citizens of Tyre and Sidon would have repented
of their sins. According to Molina, in order for Christ to have
made such a statement, God must be able to know what free
creatures would freely do in various circumstances; that is, God
must have middle knowledge. Once this type of knowledge is
admitted, according to Molina, the problem of future contingents can be dissolved in this way: God knows what non-

voluntary, contingent states of affairs he causes to be actual. Thus he knows the circumstances free creatures are actually put in: the sorts of material circumstances they find themselves in, the types of spiritual and material aids he provides, and so on. Through his middle knowledge God knows how, given any conditions, any creature would freely choose to act. Consequently, given his middle knowledge, and given that he knows which free creatures he makes actual and in what actual circumstances he places them, God knows what the actual free creatures will freely do. He thus has knowledge of all future (to us) contingents — both those depending on free actions and those that are nonvoluntary. Moreover, since voluntary agents under this scheme can choose other than they do, they are free. Thus, Molina argues, the doctrine of middle knowledge explains how God can know what free agents will do without compromising their freedom. Molina's view is imaginative and very intriguing. But before analyzing it, I want to examine Molina's comments on Scotus' and Aquinas' views about future contingents.

Contrary to the views of some scholars,[18] my position is that Molina read and understood Aquinas' position on God's knowledge of future contingents. He disagreed with the solution, but this disagreement was built on a basic understanding of Aquinas' arguments. Having studied and commented on Aquinas' writings, especially the *Summa Contra Gentiles,* Molina realized that Aquinas taught that God knows future contingents in two different ways:

> ... Thomas maintains that, because God knows all contingents not only as they are in their causes but also as each of them is in act in itself according to its existence, God certainly and infallibly knows all contingents as they are present to him according to their existence, and that nonetheless the contingents remain future in time in comparison with their causes.[19]

According to Molina, Aquinas posits the two different ways of knowing future contingents — through their causes and through their presentiality to the eternal now — for this reason: God can know for certain what non-voluntary agents do on the basis of his own causality. Since non-voluntary agents are not free agents, God's causal activity can determine their actions without destroying any freedom they have. Of course, so long as God retains the power to cause other than he in fact causes, the effects he causally brings about are contingent and his determining activity does not render them necessary. The case of the contingent actions of free agents is very different, however. If God knows their future actions through his causality, this is tantamount to claiming that God causes the free agents to do what they do, and, consequently, the free agents would not be free. God must, therefore, know the future actions of free agents in some way other than through his causality. Aquinas argues that God knows the future actions of free agents by these actions being present to God in the eternal now. Since God sees the actions, his knowledge of them is certain. Moreover, since he sees the actions as they are present to him, the actions are free. This summary and explanation of Aquinas' position clearly reveals a careful study of Aquinas' writings.

Molina read Scotus' account of God's knowledge of future contingents very carefully as well. In commenting on Scotus' view, Molina claims that Scotus is right to say that the divine ideas alone are not sufficient to explain God's knowledge of future contingents. The divine will must be involved in God's knowledge.[20] Molina undoubtedly supports Scotus on this point in order to give additional strength to his own doctrine of middle knowledge. According to this doctrine, God knows what actual creatures would do because God wills them to exist in particular circumstances. Thus, for Molina, God's willing activity is a very important component of his solution to the problem of future contingents.

From Molina's endorsement of Scotus' position one might expect him to side with Scotus in his criticism of Aquinas' theory of omniscience. Molina does not do this, however. Part of the reason is that Molina does not think that Scotus sufficiently appreciates Aquinas' position. Indeed, Molina thinks that Scotus fails to understand two important aspects of Aquinas' position: the doctrine of presentiality and the role of secondary causes.

In *De Scientia Dei,* Disputatio 6, Molina discusses what he takes to be Scotus' objection to Aquinas' doctrine of presentiality.[21] Surprisingly, Molina's major objection to Scotus' criticism of Aquinas' notion is that Scotus thinks that whatever is present to God's eternity must exist in a time different from real or imagined time.[22] It is difficult to determine what Molina means by his objection. On the one hand, he might mean that Scotus is criticizing Aquinas for postulating a third type of time midway between temporal time and eternity. If this is Molina's point, it is a misreading of Scotus' argument since Scotus, in discussing Aquinas' theory, never talks about such a time. On the other hand, Molina might be claiming that Scotus thinks Aquinas is committed to saying that future contingents must occur at a temporal time other than the future for his theory to work. This is probably the objection he has in mind, for Scotus, as we have seen, does say that on Aquinas' theory future contingents would either not occur or be twice produced.[23] Moreover, this reading is confirmed by the specific Scotistic arguments Molina examines in this section of *De Scientia Dei*.

In all, Molina treats five different arguments, the most interesting of which are the first, the third, and the fourth. The first objection states that future contingents cannot coexist with God's eternity, and is drawn from two separate claims: the claim that in order for something to coexist with an existing thing, it must also exist; and the claim that future contingents, since they are future, do not exist.[24] The third objection also concerns coexistence. According to Aquinas' theory, past and future both coexist with the eternal now. It follows from this that they coexist with each other. But it is obvious that past and future cannot coexist. From this it follows that they both cannot coexist with a common third, i.e., the eternal now.[25] The fourth objection is in a very different spirit but is, perhaps, the most interesting. If past, present, and future are all present in eternity, contradictories will be simultaneously true in eternity. For example, "Adam is"—which was true long ago in the past—and "Adam is not"—which is true today—would both be true. This, of course, is absurd.[26]

In answering these objections, Molina cites the explanation of Cajetan (although he claims that Cajetan was not the first to present it).[27] This explanation consists in pointing out that a verb in the present tense has an ambiguous signification: it can signify the temporal present, and it can signify the eternal present. Thus, when Aquinas claims that the past and future coexist, this can be taken in two different ways. If it is taken to mean that the past and future occur in the temporal present, it is obviously false. If, however, it is taken to mean that the past and future occur together in the eternal now, it is true, since there is no succession in the eternal now, and so whatever is in the eternal now occurs together with whatever else is in the eternal now. According to Molina, once it is understood that there is a

distinction between existence in the temporal present and existence in the eternal now, the five Scotistic objections are easily
answered.

In his response to the first objection, Molina claims that it is
true that in temporal time only things that exist at present can
be said to coexist with some other presently existing thing. But
in the now of eternity things that do not exist in the temporal
present can coexist with things that occur in the temporal past
and future.[28] The third objection, according to Molina, is true if
one thinks of it as stating that the past and the future, by virtue
of coexisting with the eternal now, coexist in the temporal
present. But it is false when one realizes that it only states that
past and future coexist in the eternal now. Since the eternal now
has no succession or duration, all that is found in it must be
found together.[29] The same theme is stressed in Molina's response
to the fourth objection. According to Molina, two sentences like
"Socrates is sitting" and "Socrates is not sitting" are contradictory if they are both true at the same instant of temporal time.
The eternal now, however, is present to many different instants
of temporal time. From the fact that two sentences are true in
the eternal now, it thus does not follow that the sentences are
true at the same temporal instant. Therefore, two sentences true
in the eternal now that seem to be contradictory are not really contradictory after all. They pertain to different temporal instants.[30]
Molina uses similar strategies in replying to the other Scotistic
objections he treats. The general impression one derives from
Molina's remarks is that he thinks Scotus does not understand
the relationship between temporal time and eternity since Scotus
constantly tries to put the eternal present into the temporal
present.

Molina also thinks that Scotus failed to understand the role
played in the Thomistic position by secondary causes. He presents this criticism in the context of discussing Scotus' claim
that philosophers who state both that there are contingencies
and that God acts necessarily contradict themselves.[31] Scotus
defends this claim in his discussion of God's knowledge of
future contingents. If we return briefly to his discussion, we
recall that Scotus thinks that there could be contingencies only
if God willed contingently. He claims this because he thought
that every cause in the universe is part of some essential order
having God as its first element. If God were to act necessarily,
every cause in every essential order would also act necessarily.

Only if God acts contingently would contingencies exist in the universe.

As Molina correctly saw, on Scotus' position, all secondary causes move insofar as they are moved by God.[32] According to Scotus, this is true also of human wills, which are voluntary secondary causes. This view, however, seemed to Molina neither true nor safe,[33] since it entails that God causes human wills to will what they will, which robs men of their free will.

In order to explain how contingencies can exist in the universe, even though God acts necessarily, Molina expounds and endorses what he takes to be a Thomistic position.[34] It is wrong, according to Molina's understanding of the position, to think that either God or a secondary agent is the total cause of any effect; on the contrary, God and the secondary cause are both partial causes. This means, of course, that God's bringing about an effect through a secondary cause depends upon the activity of the secondary cause.[35] In the case of non-voluntary secondary causes, God controls the activities of the secondary causes and so the contribution of such secondary causes is minimal. But the case is very different with free secondary causes. Given that these agents are free, God cannot, without eliminating their freedom, determine how they will act. God can co-act with a free secondary cause by guaranteeing the existence and power of these causes, but he cannot determine these causes.[36] This being the case, whatever God brings about through the activities of free secondary causes depends upon the free and contingent actions of these agents. Even if God acts necessarily, so long as there are free secondary causes, contingency exists in the world. The contingency would result from the contingent acts of free secondary causes.

According to Molina, Scotus fails to understand that free secondary causes must not be subject to God's determination. Indeed, according to Molina, Scotus' analysis of God's knowledge of future contingents is dangerous to the faith for precisely this reason, i.e., Scotus' analysis eliminates the free will of human beings—contrary to the testimony of scripture, and to the proclamations of various councils.[37] Molina, therefore, rejects Scotus' overall analysis of God's knowledge of future contingents.

Molina is, of course, correct in claiming that Scotus in his solution to the problem of future contingents assumes that God determines human wills. For Scotus, such determination is the basis upon which God knows what human beings will do. Moreover, Molina is also right in saying that Aquinas' claims about the activities of free secondary causes are very important to Aquinas' solution to the problem of future contingents. As Molina saw, because God, according to Aquinas, cannot determine the actions of free secondary agents, Aquinas had to postulate that the activities of free secondary agents are present to the eternal now. Even though Molina saw all this and defended Aquinas against Scotus on a number of points, Molina rejected as inadequate Aquinas' solution to the problem of future contingents for several reasons. These reasons are advanced in *De Scientia Dei,* Disputatio Seven.[38] Although Molina advances six objections, I wish to discuss only the three most compelling.

The first objection is the most successful. According to Aquinas' analysis, God knows what contingents depending on the actions of free agents occur by those contingents being present to his eternity. He cannot know them through his causality because this would eliminate their freedom. But it then follows that God cannot know the possible but unactual actions of free creatures. He cannot know them by their being present to his eternity; since they are unactual, they cannot be present to his eternity. Obviously, he cannot know them through his causality, for this would deprive the free actions of their freedom. Thus, on Aquinas' position, God cannot know these possible but unactual actions. Yet, it is obvious from the story of Chorazin and Betsaida that God has such knowledge, for, in that story, Christ knows what the citizens of Tyre and Sidon would have done if the miracles and great works had been performed in their city. This is an effective criticism of the Thomistic position.[39]

Molina's second criticism is closely related to the first. He thinks that God would be imperfect if he were unable to know what a free agent would freely do under various conditions, e.g., if a free agent had a longer life or if the agent were given more divine aids. Yet, the Thomistic position seems committed to saying that God has this defect.[40]

In his fourth objection,[41] Molina claims that God knows all things merely by looking into his own essence without the influence or existence of anything outside his essence. In fact, it would be demeaning for God to require anything outside his own essence for his knowledge, as Aquinas himself admits. Yet, on Molina's understanding of Aquinas' doctrine of omniscience, God requires something outside his essence for his knowledge. On Aquinas' theory, God can know through his essence the free actions of human beings only if these actions actually exist and are present to the eternal now. If they do not actually exist and are not consequently reflected in the divine essence, as we have seen above in his first criticism of Aquinas, they are not known by God. God thus requires something outside his own essence in order for him to know all things, and, for both Aquinas and Molina, this demeans God.

It is interesting that Molina's own doctrine of middle knowledge is not subject to this objection. On Molina's doctrine, God knows without reference to the world what agents would do in a variety of circumstances. He also knows without reference to the world what circumstances he makes actual, since he knows them by virtue of willing them to be actual. Given these two facts, God, according to Molina, knows what actual free agents will do in the actual world, and he knows these actions without depending on the existence of the actual world.

Disputatio 7 makes it very clear that Molina does not endorse Aquinas' position; because he finds Aquinas' analysis of God's omniscience inadequate, he rejects it. His arguments against Aquinas are, for the most part, different from Scotus'. Moreover, it is clear also that Molina rejects Scotus' analysis because he thinks that this analysis deprives men of free will. Molina therefore formulates his own solution to the problem. There are, however, difficulties with this solution. In the next section, by contrasting Molina's solution with Scotus', I hope to clarify further the positions of the two men.

MOLINA'S DOCTRINE OF MIDDLE KNOWLEDGE

Molina's chief objection to Scotus' theory, as we have seen, is that it takes away the ability of men to perform free actions. According to Molina, 'freedom' is to be understood in this way:

> ... we call that [agent] free which, having all that is required for acting in its power, can act or not act, or do something or its opposite. And this faculty of acting or of doing something or its opposite when all that is required for acting is given is called liberty.[42]

Molina says this is the sense of freedom that is opposed to necessitation. There are other senses of freedom, e.g., the liberty

opposed to coercion and the liberty opposed to servitude.[43]
Nevertheless, the definition offered above is the one he endorses.

Given this definition of 'freedom', it is easy to see why Molina
thinks Scotus' position eliminates free will: On Scotus' position,
the actions of human beings are determined. Of course, Scotus,
as we have seen, does not think that this determination is in
conflict with the freedom of agents. This is because Scotus
offers a definition of 'freedom' different from Molina's.

It is interesting that Molina did not understand Scotus to
have offered a different definition of 'freedom'. I think that there
are at least two explanations for this oversight. In the first
place, Molina was attempting to combat the doctrines of the
Protestant reformers. Both Calvin and Luther claim that God's
necessitation is compatible with the freedom of human beings,
since they define 'freedom' as the liberty of spontaneity. Molina
undoubtedly would be very hesitant to read Scotus as putting
forth what he thought to be a Protestant doctrine. Secondly, I
think that there is a problem of vocabulary. If we briefly return
to Scotus' discussions of freedom, we recall that Scotus separates abilities from the exercise of abilities. In fact, he allows
that an agent might possess an ability that he might never have
an opportunity to exercise. Molina, on the other hand, does not
separate abilities from their exercise. For Molina, one has an
ability if and only if one has opportunity to exercise it. An
ability that will not be exercised because of the continual interference of an external agent is not an ability at all for Molina.
When he read Scotus, Molina undoubtedly read Scotus through
his own terminology. He thus assumes that Scotus shares his
understanding of abilities and his libertarian notion of freedom.
Consequently, he sees Scotus' analysis of God's knowledge of
future contingents as violating what he assumes is Scotus' definition of 'freedom' and rejects his analysis. Perhaps the incorpo-
ration of Molina's interpretation of Scotus in the subsequent
literature helps to explain why so many people view Scotus as a
libertarian.[44] In any event, had Molina understood Scotus' definition of 'freedom', he could only have claimed that Scotus'
position on God's knowledge of future contingents is in conflict
with the definition of 'freedom' he himself endorses.

Given Molina's criticisms of Scotus, one might wonder whether
Molina's own theory conflicts with his favored definition of
'freedom'. In his extremely interesting article, "Middle Knowledge and the Problem of Evil," Robert Adams discusses the

relationship between middle knowledge and human freedom.[45] His overall strategy is to present the defenders of middle knowledge with a dilemma: Either the grounds for the truth of propositions known through middle knowledge are necessitating and thus the actions of the agents in question are not free, or the grounds are non-necessitating in which case the propositions are only probable, and not indubitable, as is claimed by the adherents of middle knowledge. To advance this dilemma, Adams focuses on Molina's and Suarez's analysis of the biblical story of David at Keilah.

According to Adams, Molina and Suarez take the story to show that God knows the following two propositions to be true:

(1) If David stayed in Keilah, Saul would besiege the city.
(2) If David stayed in Keilah and Saul besieged the city, the men of Keilah would surrender David to Saul.

But how can God know these to be true? According to Adams, a number of possibilities suggest themselves. In the first place, it might be claimed that David's staying in Keilah logically entails that Saul besiege the city, and that David's staying and Saul's besieging logically entail that the Keilahites surrender David. If so, given that God knows that David stays in the city, he would know that Saul would besiege the city and that the Keilahites would surrender David. But this analysis does not preserve the libertarian freedom of Saul or the Keilahites. Simply, if there is a logical connection between David's staying and Saul's besieging, then once David stays Saul cannot do other than besiege.

Adams also addresses the suggestion that Saul's besieging Keilah follows by causal necessity from David's staying there, together with a number of other features of the situation which in fact obtained.[46] Adams gives this suggestion short shrift, claiming that this causal necessity is also inconsistent with Saul's freedom. If David's staying at Keilah causally necessitates Saul's besieging the city, then, if David stays, Saul cannot do other than besiege the city.

According to Adams, once we have eliminated logical and causal guarantees, only the actual intentions, desires, and characters of Saul and the Keilahites present themselves as grounds for the truth of (1) and (2).[47] That is, one might argue that (1) is true by virtue of its relation to Saul's intentions and that (2) is true by virtue of its relation to the character and desires of the men of Keilah. Unfortunately, the truth of neither (1) nor (2) is guaranteed in this way, for men can act out of character or can act otherwise than their intentions indicate. According to Adams, what is shown is, at best, that:

(5) If David stayed in Keilah, Saul would *probably* besiege the city, and

(6) If David stayed in Keilah and Saul besieged the city, the men of Keilah would *probably* surrender David to Saul.

But such probabilistic propositions are not what adherents of middle knowledge claim God knows; according to them, he knows *infallibly* what agents would do. Thus we have Adams's dilemma: Either the grounds for the truth of propositions like (1) and (2) are necessitating and the actions of the agents in question are not free, or the grounds are non-necessitating, in which case the propositions are only probable and are not indubitable.

With his usual thoroughness, Adams points out that Molina and Suarez offer specific defenses of the possibility of middle knowledge.[48] The best construction Adams can give of Suarez's explanation is to see Suarez as claiming there are certain properties of God's ideas of agents. Unfortunately, according to Adams, this set-up compromises the freedom of these agents.

Molina's explanation that God has "supercomprehension" is quite different. In brief, the claim that God supercomprehends created free wills means that God understands them so well that he knows what they would do under various possible circumstances even though what they would do is not there, objectively, to be known. Adams's dismissal of Molina's explanation is direct:

> But that is impossible. The problem to be solved is how the relevant subjunctive conditionals can be true, and nothing that may be said about the excellence of God's cognitive powers contributes anything to the solution of that problem.[49]

In the rest of his article, Adams supports this comment by analyzing the types of conditionals involved in middle knowledge. His analysis is provocative and effective. He shows, for example,

how on a possible worlds analysis the truth of relevant subjunc-
tives cannot be known early enough in the order of explanation
of God's actions to explain his decisions to create what he
creates.[50] While I agree with Adams's discussion, I think more
can be said about Molina's notion of supercomprehension.

In general, it appears that Molina discusses the notion of
supercomprehension because he thinks that there is a middle
ground between logical and causal necessitation and the mere
probabilities involved with people's characters, intentions, and
desires. Just what this middle ground is, unfortunately, is not
clear in Molina's writing. What it is supposed to do, of course, is
very clear: It gives grounds for God's knowledge of the truth of
(1) and (2) that guarantee God's knowledge but do not also
necessitate the actions of the free agents in question. Although I
am very doubtful that such a middle ground exists, for the
moment I want to grant its existence and allow it as the basis of
God's supercomprehension. As it turns out, however, even this
middle ground is inconsistent with a libertarian notion of freedom.
To see this, let us return to the case of David at Keilah.

For the sake of convenience, let us focus on the claim that
David's staying would result in Saul's besieging [proposition
(1) above]. Let us also simplify matters by saying that David's
staying and other attendant features of the situation (his men
deciding to stay on, his announcing the decision to stay while
drinking wine from a sheepskin, and so on) obtain at t_0, and
that Saul's besieging would obtain at t_5. Given this set-up, what
God knows through his middle knowledge is that, given the
circumstances at t_0 (David's staying and so on), Saul at t_5
would besiege Keilah.

Faced with this situation, Molina would, of course, claim that
Saul's act of besieging would be free.[51] But if Saul's action is
free in a libertarian sense, he must be able at t_5 not to besiege
the city even though the circumstances at t_0 had obtained.
Given God's middle knowledge of the situation, Saul's being
able at t_5 not to besiege is equivalent to Saul's being able at t_5
either (1) to change the circumstances that occurred at t_0, or (2)
to make God not hold a belief he holds, or (3) to make God hold
a false belief. It is clear, I think, that Saul cannot affect God's
belief concerning what would follow given certain antecedent
circumstances; he cannot change it or render it false. Nor can
Saul at t_5 affect the past circumstance at t_0. Thus, given that
God knows that David's staying at Keilah would result in Saul's

besieging, Saul cannot do otherwise than besiege if David stays. Hence, if God knows (1) to be true, Saul is not free in a libertarian sense. This is contrary to Molina's claims.

It is important, I think, to emphasize certain points about my argument. I have not assumed that David's staying under the circumstances obtaining at t_0 causally or logically entail that Saul besiege at t_5. I have assumed merely that which Molina himself assumes: that God knows through his supercomprehension the truth of (1). Moreover, I do not assume that the circumstances I describe as obtaining at t_0 are the only circumstances that could obtain. On the contrary, any number of different circumstances could obtain. For example, at t_0 David might refrain from drinking and might decide to depart. Or he might first decide to stay and then change his mind. Whatever the circumstances, however, on Molina's view—that God knows what any free creature would do in any circumstance—there is a relevant conditional parallel to (1), e.g., if David does not decide to stay in the city, Saul would not besiege the city. And it is the truth of these conditionals (pace Adams), based on the middle ground between necessity and probability, and God's knowledge of them that compromise the libertarian freedom of agents.

My view of Molina's doctrine may seem surprising. Aquinas, for example, argues that if God's beliefs are outside time, his knowledge of the future actions of creatures would not be deterministic. Simply put, since the actions of creatures are present to God in the eternal now, creatures can act any way they wish and God would still know the actions. Of course, if God's knowledge is in time and prior to the actions of agents, his knowledge of actions would be deterministic. In the case at hand, however, we have a mixed situation. God is assumed by Molina to be outside time. Yet he holds a belief about the connection between an event in time (the circumstances of David's staying) and an event occurring at a later time (Saul besieging). It is because he holds this belief that he knows what Saul would do if he creates the appropriate circumstances. He does not, on Molina's theory of middle knowledge, know what Saul would do because Saul's action is present to the eternal now. And this fact makes all the difference. While Aquinas' doctrine of the presentiality of actions (if it makes sense) is not deterministic, Molina's doctrine of middle knowledge is deterministic, and thus violates a libertarian sense of 'freedom'.

It is the mixed nature of Molina's position that renders my

argument immune from the type of attack Plantinga offers in *God, Freedom, and Evil.*[52] In line with this discussion, Plantinga would argue that Saul's being able at t_5 not to beseige Keilah is *not* equivalent to Saul's being able at t_5 either (1) to change the circumstances that occurred at t_0, or (2) to make God not hold a belief he holds, or (3) to make God hold a false belief. In particular, Plantinga would urge that (2) should be changed into:

> (2′) to do something such that if he had done it, then God would not have held a belief that he in fact did hold,

and that (3) should be changed into:

> (3′) to do something such that if he had done it, then a belief that God did hold at t_1 would have been false.

But once we understand (2′) and (3′), there is nothing contradictory about Saul so acting. Saul is thus able to act other than he does and is free in a libertarian sense.

In formulating Plantinga's possible reply, I assume that he would not wish to reformulate (1) into:

> (1′) to do something such that if he had done it, then the circumstances that occurred at t_0 would not have occurred at t_0.

I say this because what the past circumstances at t_0 could have been is not relevant to what Saul can do at t_5 given what in fact occurs at t_0. That is, given that, for example, David decided at t_0 to stay in Keilah, Saul can do nothing at t_5 to make this not the case; he cannot, in short, change the past even though the past could have been other than it is. This seems uncontroversial, as Aquinas pointed out in his analysis of God's omniscience.

Yet, if the fact that the past cannot change once it has occurred is uncontroversial, we must wonder about Plantinga's championing of (2′) and (3′). Surely, one of the circumstances occurring at t_0 is the fact that God holds a belief about the relationship between the circumstances at t_0 and the events at t_5. Granting this, however, what belief God could have held at t_0 is irrelevant to what Saul can do at t_5 given what God in fact believes at t_0. For Saul cannot at t_5 act so that the past is other than it is in fact at t_0. Similar considerations apply to (3′) and consequently

Plantinga's possible objection does not undermine my argument against Molina.

Similarly, I do not think a distinction between "hard" and "soft" facts about the past saves Molina's position.[53] Given that God in fact holds a belief about the circumstances at t_0 and the events at t_5 and that the circumstances obtain at t_0, his belief is a hard fact relative to t_5.

Having pointed out the conflict between middle knowledge and a libertarian sense of freedom, it is important to point out a crucial difference between Scotus' and Molina's theories of omniscience. On Molina's theory, the identity of a possible person is not as strongly tied to the actions the person performs as in Scotus' theory. For Molina, the David who decides to stay in Keilah and the David who decides to leave are one and the same person; they differ only in the decisions they make. The possible David God contemplates in the eternal now could have different histories and still be the same possible person in each history. In a more contemporary vocabulary, we would say that Molina thinks that the same person is found in a variety of possible worlds. This assumption, I think, is part of the reason Molina thinks that a person that God knows would perform some action could perform another action. Scotus' notion of the possible person, on the other hand, is very strongly tied to the actions the person performs, for the possible person is just the set of actions he performs if created. Thus the possible David who decides to stay at Keilah is different from the possible David who leaves. The two possible Davids are similar, but they are not the same person. Restated in contemporary terms, Scotus thinks that each possible person is world bound, i.e., that each possible person can exist in only one possible world. Thus, God's creation of one possible person rather than another entails the actions of that person in the actual world. It is obvious, then, that Scotus must define 'freedom' in some way differently from Molina. If he did not, his view of possible persons would entail that it is impossible for anyone to be free.

Molina is generally a careful reader of both Scotus and Aquinas. He judiciously analyzes the positions of the two men and points out the difficulties. Unfortunately, he misunderstands one of Scotus' key doctrines, i.e., Scotus' notion of freedom. Moreover, his doctrine of middle knowledge has a number of inherent difficulties. Nevertheless, Molina's doctrine does throw light on aspects of Scotus' own theory. For example, it is clear that

Scotus' separation of abilities from the exercise of abilities is a crucial component of Scotus' non-libertarian view of freedom. Also, Scotus, unlike Molina, regards possible persons as world bound. In addition, it is clear from Molina's discussion of Scotus that Scotus' second attack on Aquinas' position (that God would not know all actualities) is much stronger than his first (that the distinctions among past, present, and future collapse). As we shall see, the theories of the next person to be examined, Leibniz, also help to clarify Scotus' position.

5 Leibniz on God's Knowledge and Freedom

INTRODUCTION

When disputes between the Dominicans and the Jesuits over the issue of free will had reached a fever pitch, the Pope intervened and forbade further debate.[1] Needless to say, his proclamation failed to quell the controversy, and students of philosophy as well as students of theology continued to dispute the issues. Among the most influential contributors to this debate was Thomas Hobbes.

In 1652, Hobbes wrote his treatise *Of Liberty and Necessity* in response to a work by the Bishop of Londonderry.[2] A few years later, his work *The Questions Concerning Liberty, Necessity, and Chance* appeared.[3] This second work analyzes and defends the claims of the first, and so the two present a unified view.

Hobbes was thoroughly familiar with the controversies concerning God's knowledge of contingent events and the nature of free will. In general, he criticizes the positions of the "schoolmen" for their obfuscating language and distinctions; in particular, he claims that Scotus wrote things about free will that not even Scotus himself could understand.[4] Hobbes, however, favors the positions of the Protestant reformers and especially their views on free will.

Hobbes, who found the liberty of indifference to be a contradictory notion,[5] equates freedom with the liberty of spontaneity: "For he is free to do a thing, that may do it if he have the will to do it, and may forebear, if he have the will to forebear."[6] Given this definition of 'freedom', an agent necessitated in an action remains free relative to it as long as he wills to perform the action. For Hobbes, such a notion of freedom is the only possible definition, given that God knows and wills all things. According to Hobbes, if God is omniscient, all things must occur necessarily, for if anything could be other than it is, God could be mistaken, which is absurd.[7] Such necessitation is, of course, in conflict with the liberty of indifference, a point which Hobbes repeatedly emphasizes.

Hobbes' identification of freedom with the liberty of spontaneity is not simple, for it involves a number of subtle complications. For example, Hobbes distinguishes 'liberty' from the 'liberty of spontaneity'. Since 'liberty' is merely the "absence of all the impediments to action that are not contained in the nature and intrinsical quality of the agent,"[8] even a river flowing down its channel may be said to have liberty. Yet, the river cannot be said to have liberty of spontaneity, since this type of liberty is confined to living creatures. Moreover, Hobbes claims that an action that is free by virtue of the liberty of spontaneity is a voluntary action, and he also links a voluntary action with an action that is done from deliberation.[9]

Hobbes' opinions and arguments influenced such English philosophers as John Locke and David Hume. They were studied by Gottfried Wilhelm Leibniz, as well, who incorporated some of them into his own discourse upon the problem of the relationship between God's omniscience and human freedom.

Leibniz struggled with this problem throughout his life, beginning with *Catholic Demonstrations* (1669), continuing through his major work on the problem, the *Theodicy* (1709), and beyond. He was well acquainted with the history of the controversies surrounding the problem, having been schooled in scholastic philosophy and having read Suarez's *Disputationes Metaphysicae*. And his remarks about the doctrine of middle knowledge reveal his comprehension of his predecessors.[10] He saw major inconsistencies, which he attempted to resolve within his philosophical framework. It is interesting that, although certain aspects of his solution cannot be understood outside this framework, the general solution he offers is strikingly similar to that presented by Duns Scotus. Thus, while Hobbes may have found Scotus incomprehensible, Leibniz clearly did not. On the contrary, he found much of value in Scotus' works. Due to the similarity of the positions of the two men, Leibniz's discussion of God's knowledge helps to illuminate Scotus' writings. As I shall argue, however, Leibniz's theory is undone by his definition of 'freedom'.

LEIBNIZ ON MIDDLE KNOWLEDGE

At the beginning of the main part of the *Theodicy*, Leibniz lists two difficulties intrinsic to Christianity that he thought needed to be addressed.[11] The first is the apparent incompatibility between man's freedom and the activities of the divine nature; the second is that God seems to participate too directly in evil. This second is, of course, the problem of evil, and much of the *Theodicy* is directed toward resolving it. Leibniz's discussion of the problem of evil is both provocative and innovative, anticipating many of the arguments made by contemporary writers. The *Theodicy* also offers, primarily in its first section and subsequent appendices, an extended treatment of the first problem, the compatibility of freedom and God's omniscience.

Leibniz had obviously studied extensively the dispute between the Dominicans and the Jesuits on the issue of man's freedom. He often refers to this debate and frequently invokes the writings of its principals: Molina, Bañes, Alvarez. His own views on the debate are concentrated in paragraphs thirty-nine to forty-nine of the *Theodicy*. As we shall see, Leibniz's views are colored by his own solution to the problem.

After summarizing the debate and listing Molina's three types of divine knowledge, Leibniz divides the debaters into two groups.[12] On the one side is the Jesuit Molina, and his disciples. According to this group, God knows what free men would do of their own accord if placed in various circumstances. This type of knowledge is not to be confused with God's knowledge of possibilities (called "knowledge of mere intelligence") or with his knowledge of actuals (called "knowledge of intuition"). Rather, the conditional knowledge (called "middle knowledge") is mediate between these two and is the basis upon which God knows the future free actions of free individuals. In the opposing group is the Dominican Bañes, and his followers. Leibniz calls this group the "predeterminators" because these men maintain that God knows future free actions through his predetermination of these actions.

In reviewing these two groups, Leibniz offers what he takes to be the major criticisms of the two positions. The first criticism of the Molinists we have met before:

> For what foundation can God have for seeing what the people of Keilah would do? A simple contingent and free act has nothing in itself to yield a principle of certainty, unless one look upon it as predetermined by the decrees of God, and by the causes that are dependent upon them. Consequently the difficulty existing in actual free actions will exist also in conditional free actions. . . . [13]

The criticism is straightforward. If the actual free actions can be known only through predetermination, possible free actions can also be known only through predetermination. Hence, explaining God's knowledge of future, actual free actions by means of future possible actions will not be helpful. Leibniz evidently takes this line of reasoning to be an effective critique of the Molinist position.

His second criticism of the Molinists centers on the Molinist doctrine of freedom. Leibniz claims that Molina and his followers, as well as many Thomistic thinkers, identify freedom with the liberty of indifference.[14] On Leibniz's understanding, this principle is the claim that, for an agent to be free relative to a certain action, the agent must be equally disposed towards the action and its opposite. Needless to say, this is a misunderstanding of the liberty of indifference, for it is concerned with abilities and not dispositions. Thus Leibniz's dismissals of the doctrine lack force. His unsubstantiated claim that it is an empirical fact that agents are not equally disposed towards actions and their opposites does not challenge the liberty of indifference. This is also true for his curious contention that the doctrine runs afoul of his principle of sufficient reason. According to this principle, there must be an explanation for all actions. If an agent is equally disposed towards two alternatives, on Leibniz's account, there can be no explanation for his choice. Obviously, Leibniz is here making the implausible assumption that only dispositions can enter into explanations of actions. Even more puzzling is

his claim that the liberty of indifference conflicts with his principle of the identity of indiscernibles (if two entities have all the
same properties, they must be the same entity). According to
Leibniz an agent can be equally disposed towards two options
only if the options were completely identical; but then they
would be one rather than two.[15] It is mysterious, however, why
Leibniz assumes that the strength of dispositions is so directly
linked to the nature of their objects.

It is interesting that Leibniz's criticism of the second group—
the predeterminators—does not undermine the basic predeter-
minist claim that God knows future free actions only through
his predetermination of these actions. His criticism of the
predeterminators is that the group (or at least a contemporary
subgroup of it) posits that God must constantly interact with
creatures to predetermine their actions.[16] This claim is repug-
nant to Leibniz. According to him, God has set forth all that is
necessary for the operation of the world, so that he need not
intervene to keep the world functioning. Leibniz endorses this
claim so strongly that elsewhere in his writings he claims that
miracles, defined as unplanned and mysterious interventions by
God, do not occur.[17]

Despite his disagreements with the positions of the Molinists
and the predeterminators, Leibniz remarks that he finds truth
on both sides. In order to see this, however, one must endorse
one of his own philosophical doctrines: that there is an infinity
of possible worlds.

Leibniz regards the world in which we live as the actual
world. This is the world God has chosen to create. There are,
however, many other worlds God could have created, but since
he did not choose to create them, they remain merely possible.
These possible but unactual worlds can be seen as variations
on the real world.[18] For instance, in the actual world Saul did
not lay siege to Keilah to capture David since David chose not to
hide in Keilah. There is, however, a conceivable world—a possible
world—that closely resembles our world except that in that
world Saul does besiege Keilah.[19] Obviously, most of the events
in the actual world could have been otherwise, and could have
been otherwise in an unlimited number of ways. Consequently,
Leibniz maintains that there is an infinite number of possible
worlds.

Once one accepts Leibniz's notion, it becomes clear that the
Molinists are correct in asserting that God can know both the

actual and the possible actions of free creatures. Every action, whether actual or possible, is a component of a complete possible world. Even though there is an infinite number of possible worlds, God knows each one of them in complete detail since he has an infinite intellect. He thus knows every possible action that a free creature can perform. Given that he knows what possible world he makes actual, God also knows which of these possible actions would be actual.[20] He thus knows all actual and possible actions of free creatures.

In terms of the predeterminators, Leibniz says:

> And if I am for the Molinists in the first part, I am for the predeterminators in the second, provided always that predetermination be taken as not necessitating. In a word, I am of opinion that the will is always more inclined towards the course it adopts, but that it is never bound by necessity to adopt it. That it will adopt this course is certain, but it is not necessary.[21]

It is clear from this passage that Leibniz thinks that the predeterminators are right in claiming that God knows future free actions through his predetermination of these actions. It is also clear from this passage that he thinks that God's predetermination of future free actions is not inconsistent with their freedom—contrary to the claims of the Molinists. As we shall see, Leibniz's view on this is also closely connected to his doctrine of an infinity of possible worlds.

Leibniz's view of the dispute between the Dominicans and the Jesuits thus is somewhat puzzling. On the one hand, he seems to agree with the basic tenet of the Jesuits, i.e., that God can know all possible, future free actions. On the other hand, he agrees with the main contention of the Dominicans, i.e., that God knows future free actions only through his predetermining activity and this predetermination does not eliminate freedom. Leibniz thus seems to agree with opposite views about God's knowledge of future contingents. As it turns out, Leibniz can, in fact, agree with both groups, given his own solution to the problem of God's knowledge of future contingents. In order to see this, we must turn to Leibniz's solution to the problem.

LEIBNIZ ON GOD'S KNOWLEDGE OF FUTURE CONTINGENTS

In several of the letters he exchanged with Arnauld concerning his *Discourse on Metaphysics,* Leibniz affirms that possibilities, as logical constructs, are independent of God's will.[22] He expresses this point in terms of different possible Adams that God could have created. God, in fact, created one Adam. This is the one whose actions are recorded in the Bible, whose progeny includes all men, and whose actions caused the expulsion from the Garden of Eden and the stain of original sin on all his descendants. There were, however, other Adams that God could have created. For instance, he could have created an Adam who did not eat the fruit and who remained in the Garden of Eden. Each of these variations on Adam represents, for Leibniz, a possible Adam. They differ from the Adam of the Bible in that they are possibilities only; God did not choose to make them actual.

Leibniz claims that each of these possible Adams has associated with him "a complete individual concept." This individual concept consists of the notions of all the actions the being would perform if made actual. It is, in short, a complete lifestory of the individual. When God creates the Adam of the Bible, he chooses, from a number of complete lifestories, the lifestory with which we are familiar from the Bible. Since God knows the content of the lifestories of all creatures, God knows all that the Adam of the Bible would do in his lifetime.

The lifestories from which God chooses are independent of God in the sense that he does not determine their content. For example, God does not determine that the Adam of the Bible would choose to eat of the fruit or would have a wife named Eve. Nor does he determine that a possible but unactualized Adam would be an individual who, if created, would not have eaten of the fruit. As possible lifestories, these lifestories are merely combinations of possible actions, limited only by consistency and the rules of logic. Hence, the lifestories are, in a sense, ready-made and present to God. His function is merely to choose which of all the possible lifestories to make actual.

Leibniz does not, of course, think that only Adam has a complete lifestory. According to Leibniz, every being is associated with a complete individual concept. Moreover, God knows all the complete individual concepts associated with every possible being. He also knows all the possible combinations of possible beings, and Leibniz talks about this as God's knowledge of all possible worlds. These possible worlds are, of course, also independent of God in the sense that their contents are determined purely by consistency and logical rules. God's activity is to choose, from among all these possible worlds, one possible world to make actual.

Leibniz's views about complete, individual concepts and possible worlds are central to his philosophical system. For example, his views on these matters are closely tied to his solution of the mind-body problem, the doctrine of pre-established harmony.[23] According to this doctrine, the mind and body do not directly influence one another, but are, on the contrary, mutually independent. Nevertheless, whatever happens to the body is reflected in the mind, so that an agent can know what happens to his body because the soul contains within it the lifestory of the body with which it is associated. Through the lifestory the agent in question knows what happens to his body without the body actually influencing the soul. If there were no complete individual concepts and no one to ensure that the proper life-stories are harmonized with the proper incarnated souls, there would be no guarantee that the soul would reflect (and the agent know) the functions of the body.

Leibniz's views about individual complete concepts and possible worlds are essential to his solution to the problem of God's knowledge of future contingents as well. Since God knows all the contents of every possible world, he knows what any possible creature would do in any circumstance. He would know, for example, that in a certain possible world a mountain named Mount St. Helens would erupt in 1990 and that a trapper, R. J. Lurtsema, would choose to abandon his traps rather than fight through the resulting ash. Since God also knows what possible world he chooses to make actual, i.e., our possible world, he knows what future contingents actually occur.

So stated, Leibniz's solution seems very similar to what the Molinists term 'middle knowledge'. As we have seen, Leibniz did think that there was much truth in the Molinist position, but upon close examination, his position differs markedly from that of the Molinists. The Molinists fail to explain how it is that God knows what an agent would do in the future; they merely appeal to God's supercomprehension. Leibniz, on the other hand, explains how God knows the future actions. In effect, God knows the properties that a possible being has. For example, R. J.

Lurtsema has the property of abandoning his traps in 1990. This, together with many other properties, constitutes his complete lifestory. Given that a creature has such properties, the creature acts in accord with the content of these properties. Since God knows all the properties possessed by any possible creature, he knows what all actual creatures would do in the future. Of course, this theory of how God knows future contingents is strikingly similar to that posited by Scotus. It may be recalled that Scotus held that God knows all possible states of affairs through his intellect alone prior to choosing one possible, consistent set to make actual. He also held that God would know fully everything about the possibles he chooses to make actual, and that God would thus know all future events in the actual world. While Scotus did not use such notions as 'individual complete concepts' and 'possible worlds', his view can easily be recast in these terms.

The similarity between Scotus' and Leibniz's views is not surprising, since Leibniz knew of Scotus' discussion of God's knowledge of future contingents. He mentions Scotus several times in the *Theodicy,* for example. Here he talks about Scotus' rejection of Aristotle's dictum whereby all that exists, exists of necessity while it exists.[24] Later in the same work, he cites Scotus' claim that if there were no freedom in God, there would be no freedom in creatures.[25] These passages strongly suggest a familiarity with Book I, distinctions 38 and 39 of Scotus' *Commentary on the Sentences,* in which Scotus discusses the problem of future contingents. Further, in the appendix to the *Theodicy* entitled "Summary of the Controversy Reduced to Formal Arguments," Leibniz indicates that he has read Book I, distinction 47, question 11 of Scotus' *Commentary.*[26] Finally, in his early work *De Principio Individui,* Leibniz discusses Scotus' views on the principle of individuation.[27] It is clear, then, that Leibniz knew Scotus' work, and that he particularly drew upon those sections in which Scotus discusses the problem of future contingents. Although Leibniz himself was not explicit concerning his indebtedness to Scotus, that he was to some extent influenced by his writings is beyond question.

Since Leibniz's solution to the problem of future contingents is so similar to Scotus', one would expect it to exhibit similar defects. In particular, Leibniz's solution, like Scotus', seems to compromise the freedom of free agents. Leibniz foresaw this objection, and in the *Theodicy,* he remarks:

> Since, moreover, God's decree consists solely in the reso-
> lution he forms, after having compared all possible worlds,
> to choose that one which is the best, and bring it into
> existence together with all that this world contains, by
> means of the all-powerful word *Fiat,* it is plain to see that
> this decree changes nothing in the constitution of things:
> God leaves them just as they were in the state of mere
> possibility, that is, changing nothing either in their essence
> or nature, or even in their accidents, which are represented
> perfectly already in the idea of this possible world. Thus
> that which is contingent and free remains no less so
> under the decrees of God than under his prevision.[28]

The point Leibniz stresses here is that God does not, by creating them, cause creatures to do what they do. On the contrary,
he merely allows them to exist and do what they would do
(according to the contents of their complete individual concepts).
Thus, God's creative act is not deterministic. (This is a point
Scotus missed in his analysis of God's omniscience. Scotus
thought that God's creative act was deterministic, and he offered
his definition of freedom as a way to render this determination
compatible with freedom.)

Leibniz is right, of course, in saying that on his scheme God's
actualization of creatures does not determine the actions of the
creatures. But he wants further to maintain that at least some of
the creatures God creates are free, e.g., human beings. This
statement is valid, however, only if at least some of the creatures
God creates are free prior to God's creative act. If all creatures
are determined independently of God's creative activity, then,
even if God's creative act is not deterministic, God could not
create free creatures. In particular, for Leibniz to think that God
can create free creatures, he must assume that creatures are not
determined by virtue of the existence of complete individual
concepts. Arnauld, in his exchange with Leibniz, questioned
this very assumption.

Arnauld apparently did not read the whole text of the *Discourse
of Metaphysics,* but read only a schematic summary of thirty-
seven propositions (which constitute the headings of the thirty-
seven paragraphs of the *Discourse*). He objects most strenuously,
in his first letter to Count Ernst von Hessen-Rheinfels, the
intermediary in the exchange of letters, to Article 13, in which
Leibniz says:

As the individual concept of each person includes once for all everything which can ever happen to him, in it can be seen *a priori* the evidences or the reasons for the reality of each event and why one happened sooner than the other. But these events, however certain, are nevertheless contingent being based on the free choice of God and of his creatures. It is true that their choices always have their reasons but they incline to the choices under no compulsion of necessity.[29]

To this proposition Arnauld replies:

> If this is so, God was free, to create or not to create Adam, but supposing he decided to create him, all that has since happened to the human race or which will ever happen to it has occurred and will occur by a necessity more than fatal.[30]

The objection is straightforward. If the complete individual concept contains notions of all that a creature can do, then the creature must do what its individual concept indicates. Presumably, if it did not, it would not be the creature it is. Unfortunately, Arnauld clouds his objection by linking it to the claim that God is not free to create the type of Adam he wants.[31] Leibniz spends considerable time answering this problem, but he also responds to Arnauld's more compelling objection. In his letter of July 14, 1686, Leibniz offers this reply to Arnauld's claim that the complete individual concept necessitates a creature's actions:

> In order to make my reply clear, I agree that the connection of events, although it is certain, is not necessary, and that I am at liberty either to make or not to make the journey, for although it is involved in my concept that I will make it, it is also involved that I will make it freely.[32]

This response is very similar to Augustine's answer to the problem of determination through God's knowledge, and it is subject to the same response: It begs the question.[33] Leibniz cannot assume that the freedom of an action is guaranteed by the fact that the complete individual concept contains the notion "freely performs the act in question." For Arnauld is arguing that any action whose notion is in the complete individual concept is determined by that fact. Obviously, Leibniz must provide a better explanation than this of how an action whose notion is contained in a complete individual concept can be free. Following the strategy of Scotus, it would appear that the most fruitful explanation would be to clarify what is meant by 'freedom', and Leibniz does this. To see whether this move succeeds, we must investigate what he means by 'freedom'.

LEIBNIZ ON FREEDOM

An examination of the literature reveals a striking lack of unanimity about Leibniz's definition of 'freedom'. Some students of Leibniz claim, on the one hand, that he identifies freedom with logical contingency; but others regard him as equating freedom with the liberty of spontaneity. There is, in fact, evidence for both positions.

Leibniz claims in a number of places that there are at least two distinct types of necessity: absolute (sometimes called logical) necessity and hypothetical necessity. Something is absolutely necessary if it cannot be otherwise or, equivalently, if its negation is a logical contradiction. For example, that everything is identical to itself is a necessary proposition since its negation would be self-contradictory. On the other hand, something is hypothetically necessary if it is necessary given certain conditions. For example, given that John is a bachelor, it is necessary that he be unmarried. It is not absolutely necessary that he be unmarried since, obviously, he could be married. Given that he is a bachelor, however, it then is necessary that he be unmarried. From these characterizations, it is clear that everything that is only hypothetically necessary is logically contingent. That is, the hypothetically necessary will not occur if the conditions necessitating it do not obtain.

There are several passages in Leibniz's writings indicating that he regards only absolute necessity as inconsistent with freedom and that he regards what is only hypothetically necessary as free.[34] Of course, if Leibniz does identify freedom with the absence of absolute (logical) necessity, it would be obvious why he does not regard his analysis of God's knowledge as in conflict with the future free actions of agents. Since God is free to choose among an infinity of possible worlds, for any choice

God makes he could have chosen otherwise. Thus, no action a creature performs is logically necessary even if a notion of it is contained in the complete individual concept associated with the creature. Unfortunately, identifying freedom with the absence of logical necessity is not a sufficient characterization of freedom. This can easily be seen by considering the following case: Let us assume that a hypnotist has put a subject into a hypnotic trance. Let us also assume that he has made the post-hypnotic suggestion that the patient say "the devil made me do it" whenever he hears the word 'Sarasota'. After bringing the subject out of the trance, the hypnotist introduces to the subject various people who have vacationed in Florida. One couple describes their trip from Tampa to Miami through Sarasota. Upon hearing this, the subject utters "the devil made me do it."

It is clear that the subject who had been given the post-hypnotic suggestion had to utter the phrase. He really was not free; he had no choice about what he was doing. This is true even though it was not absolutely necessary that he say what he said (the hypnotist could have suggested another phrase) nor was it absolutely necessary that he be hypnotized (he could have refused to participate). In short, as Arnauld remarked to Leibniz, hypothetical necessity is often sufficient to compromise freedom:

> It does not appear to me, Monsieur, that, in speaking thus, I have confused necessitation ex hypothesi [hypothetical necessity] and absolute necessity, for I was all the time speaking only against the necessity ex hypothesi; what I find strange is, that all human events should be quite as necessary by a necessity ex hypothesi after this first supposition that God wished to create Adam, as it is necessary by the same necessity for there to be in the world a nature capable of thinking simply because he has wished to create me.[35]

Given these difficulties with identifying freedom with the lack of absolute necessity, it appears that it would be uncharitable to saddle Leibniz with such a view. This has caused many to seek in Leibniz's writings for some other definition of 'freedom'.

According to many students of Leibniz, there is considerable evidence to suggest that Leibniz identifies freedom with the liberty of spontaneity. In the *Theodicy,* for example, Leibniz

remarks several times that our souls have a "wonderful spontaneity" and that they are their own principles of action.[36] He
cites with approval Aristotle's claim that the source of our
actions is within us and that external objects have no influence
on us.[37] In his *Discourse on Metaphysics,* Leibniz states that
according to his theory of God's knowledge of future contingents,
God produces our being in such a way that thoughts arise in us
spontaneously and freely.[38] Leibniz makes similar claims in
the appendix to the *Theodicy* entitled *De Causa Dei.*

Although these passages do indicate that Leibniz links the
liberty of spontaneity with freedom, they also make it clear that
he does not wholly identify the two.[39] For example, in his
"Reflections on the Work that Mr. Hobbes Published in English
on 'Freedom, Necessity, and Chance'," Leibniz indicates that
Hobbes' definition of 'freedom' as the absence of external constraint is a very general characterization common to intelligent
and non-intelligent beings alike.[40] This remark bears an implicit
criticism. Leibniz maintains that the freedom of intelligent agents
(especially human beings) involves much more than mere freedom
from constraint, and so any theory that simply links freedom
with the liberty of spontaneity is overly simplistic.[41] Leibniz
variously describes this additional necessary constituent of freedom as intelligence, choice, or judgment.[42] In fact, in his short
work, "On Freedom," Leibniz claims:

> So I was not far from the view of those who think that all
> things are absolutely necessary; who think that security
> from compulsion is enough for freedom, even though it is
> under the rule of necessity, and who do not distinguish
> the infallible—that is, a truth which is certainly known
> from the necessary.[43]

It is obvious from this passage that Leibniz was attracted by the
theory of those who identify freedom simply with the liberty of
spontaneity. Yet, as he goes on in the same passage to explain,
he did not himself make this identification:

> But I was dragged back from this precipice by a consid-
> eration of those possibles which neither do exist, nor will
> exist, nor have existed. For if certain possibles never
> exist, then existing things are not always necessary.

This passage indicates that Leibniz does not wholly and simply identify freedom with the liberty of spontaneity, and scholars who view Leibniz as making this identification are clearly mistaken. As the passage further indicates, Leibniz understands his view of freedom to be linked with the existence of possibles. As it turns out, this link provides a key to Leibniz's theory of freedom and a way of reconciling his diverse remarks about freedom.

On the page immediately following the above passage, Leibniz writes that the nature of freedom springs from "the infinite."[44] John Hostler has recently argued that this phrase provides an essential clue to Leibniz's theory of freedom.[45] According to Hostler, the central part of Leibniz's theory is his stress on the act of choice. Freedom, on Hostler's interpretation of Leibniz, can occur only when an intelligent agent has a choice among many options. Leibniz in fact expresses this view in this passage quoted by Hostler:

> When there are many roads available one has the freedom to choose among them, the choice being determined by the fact that one would be better than another. Even when only one road is good, as when there is a bridge across a deep and swift river, one still makes a choice between the bridge and the river—though, of course, the choice is not much in doubt. But if one were in a narrow street between two high walls, there would be only one way to go: and this situation represents necessity.[46]

The fact that there are an infinite number of possible worlds that God could have created ensures that a free agent has a variety of options to choose from in relation to any action. This, according to Hostler's interpretation of Leibniz, secures the agent's freedom because he has a choice among a number of options even though he is inclined toward one over all the others.

Hostler's analysis of Leibniz's view of freedom has considerable strength. It is supported by other interpreters of Leibniz.[47] More importantly Leibniz seems to endorse it specifically: Hostler refers us to a passage in which Leibniz claims that liberty consists of three elements—intelligence, spontaneity, and contingency.[48] We have already seen what spontaneity is for Leibniz. Intelligence and contingency are linked, in that intelligence is expressed in the choice among the possible logical alternatives to a contingent action.

Another advantage of Hostler's interpretation is that it encompasses Leibniz's remarks about contingency and the liberty of spontaneity. On Hostler's interpretation, Leibniz is arguing that contingency and the liberty of spontaneity are linked with freedom but are not identical with freedom. They are necessary but not sufficient conditions of freedom. In addition, for an act to be free, the agent must be able to choose among alternatives to the action.

It thus appears that Leibniz's definition of 'freedom' is very complex. In order for an agent to be free regarding a certain action, the action must first of all be logically contingent. In addition, the agent must enjoy the liberty of spontaneity relative to the action; that is, the agent must not be externally compelled to perform the action but must choose to perform it. Finally, the agent must have a choice among alternatives to the action.

FREEDOM AND COMPLETE
INDIVIDUAL CONCEPTS

Having now elaborated Leibniz's view of freedom, we are in a position to answer the question posed at the end of the third section: Does the existence of complete individual concepts compromise the freedom of agents? Given Leibniz's definition of freedom, there will be, of course, three points to evaluate concerning this question: whether the concepts compromise contingency, whether they compromise spontaneity, and whether they compromise intelligence.

As we have seen above, the contingency of the actions of creatures apparently is not compromised by the existence of individual concepts, for as Leibniz repeatedly remarks, God could have instantiated other possible worlds than the one he in fact did instantiate. Moreover, the concepts do not compromise the creatures' spontaneity. The actions of the agent that are not externally compelled by other factors result directly from the nature of the creature. In fact, the existence of individual concepts seems to support the claim of spontaneity. But what of intelligence? As we have seen, Leibniz links intelligence with choice and holds that there is freedom only if there is a choice among options. In fact, this possibility of choice is what distinguishes human beings from brute creatures and allows us to call human beings, but not brute creatures, properly free. Does the existence of complete individual concepts compromise intelligence as Leibniz understands it?

In the *Discourse on Metaphysics,* Leibniz replies to this question: How can it be known that a man, e.g., Judas, will commit a sin? His answer is " . . . that otherwise he would not be this man."[49] This is a startling reply. In order for Judas to be Judas, he must sin. But this would imply that for Judas to do other than he does would be for Judas to be another man, which suggests that Judas, as Judas, does not really have the option of choosing differently than he chooses. Presumably the only choice Judas would have is that of not being Judas. Yet, this is not an option that he truly has. This is a choice that God has already made in choosing the actual Judas over other possible variations of Judas.

The point can, of course, be extended to all men and all actions of men. Since there is an infinity of possible worlds, it might appear that a free agent has a number of courses of actions from which he can choose. Unfortunately, given Leibniz's claim that there is a complete individual concept of each substance and that each substance must act in accordance with the content of its associated individual concept in order to be that substance, no agent can choose any course other than the one dictated by his associated complete individual concept.[50]

This criticism can be rephrased in terms of Leibniz's own notion of possible worlds. In order for a person to have a choice among various alternatives, he must be found in a number of possible worlds. For Leibniz, however, individual substances can be found in only one possible world. What we may think is the same substance in another possible world turns out to be, not the same substance, but a variation distinct from the substance in question. Indeed, given Leibniz's principle of the identity of indiscernibles and his view that each substance totally reflects the world in which it is found, the substance in a possible but unactualized world resembling a substance in the actual world must be different from the actual world substance. Otherwise the possible but unactualized world will be identical to the actual world.[51] This is, of course, absurd. But since each individual substance can be found in only one possible world, no person has a real choice among possible worlds, and so no one is free according to Leibniz's understanding of the term.

Hostler is aware of the inconsistency I present, but sees it only as an objection to Leibniz's views about contingency.[52] It is clear, I hope, that the foregoing constitutes an objection to Leibniz's view of freedom as well. In an earlier chapter of his book, however, Hostler suggests that Leibniz shows that there is a real choice:

> The criterion of intelligence, however, is more adequate for its task, since it serves to mitigate the effects of determinism. At G III, 403 [*Die Philosophischen Schriften von G. W. Leibniz,* Vol. III, p. 403], for instance, Leibniz claims that though my present choice may be determined by the situation in which I find myself, I can bring myself to choose differently when similar circumstances arise in the future.[53]

This does, of course, suggest that the reasons agents have for acting or not acting are often instrumental in determining whether agents act or not. But this, I assume, would be an aspect of an agent's spontaneity. It would not show that an agent has a real choice to do other than is indicated by his complete individual concept. The reasons the agent has for acting in circumstances resembling the circumstances of an earlier action are determined by his associated individual concept.

Leibniz's solution to the problem of God's knowledge of future contingents is similar to Scotus'. As such, it is subject to the same central question: Does the solution eliminate the freedom of free agents? Like Scotus, Leibniz sought an answer to this problem by examining and offering a non-libertarian definition of 'freedom'. Unfortunately, the definition Leibniz advances is beset by obscurities and problems. In particular, it is difficult to see how his definition moves beyond the liberty of spontaneity without running afoul of his claim that each possible person is found in only one possible world. Nevertheless, Leibniz's discussion of God's knowledge does indicate certain inadequacies of Scotus' analysis. Scotus is mistaken, for example, in assuming that God's creative activity is deterministic. The determinism involved in his system as well as Leibniz's is a determinism independent of God's creative activity. Moreover, Leibniz has presented a difficult problem for Duns Scotus' non-libertarian view of freedom: How can one separate brutes from such free agents as men in terms of freedom? Leibniz's own attempts to solve the problem are unsuccessful, but he addresses the problem, whereas Scotus does not. As we shall see in the next chapter, the legacy of Leibniz's analysis of God's knowledge, which is very similar to Scotus' analysis and part of the voluntarist tradition, is influential even today.

6 The Free Will Defense and Omniscience

INTRODUCTION

Due to the rise of the scientific method and Newtonian science, discussions about free will during the eighteenth and nineteenth centuries revolved around issues related to causal determinism. The issues discussed by Hume, Kant, Mill, and others were, of course, related to those explored by thinkers more concerned with the relationship between God's knowledge and free will. But those concerned with causal determinism generally emphasized theories about explanation in a mechanical universe rather than determination through God's knowledge or action.

Toward the middle of the twentieth century, however, there was a revival of interest in the relationship between God's knowledge and human freedom. Some of the impetus came from work in tense logic by Arthur Prior and others.[1] But much of the interest came from discussions about the problem of evil. Out of the many contributions to this problem, Alvin Plantinga's free will defense stands out in quality and interest.

The first version of the defense was published in 1965 as an article entitled "The Free Will Defence," which was included unchanged in Plantinga's *God and Other Minds*. The second version, a more technical formulation of the first, can be found in his *God, Freedom, and Evil* and *The Nature of Necessity*. Both versions have been criticized, but by far the most complete response has been offered by Nelson Pike, creating in effect a philosophical debate between the two men.[2] While it is clear that many of the positions I have treated in previous chapters underlie much of the debate concerning the first version of the defense, the second has superseded the first and I consequently turn my attention to it. My aim in this chapter is not only to evaluate Plantinga's and Pike's discussions but also to put them into historical perspective. Specifically, I hope to show that the debate concerning the second version is also related to many of the points discussed in previous chapters.

THE FREE WILL DEFENSE

According to Plantinga, a person offering the free will defense wishes to show that there is a possible world in which

(A) God is omnipotent, omniscient, and wholly good and
(Z) There is evil in the world

are both true.[3] A possible world is "a way things could have been; it is a state of affairs of some kind." For example, that God creates nothing is a state of affairs, and it constitutes a possible world. Moreover, the actual world constitutes a possible world. It, however, has a property that no other non-identical possible world shares: actuality. Of course, not just any possibility constitutes a possible world, for a possible world is a very large state of affairs. In fact, it is a maximal or complete state of affairs, i.e., a state of affairs such that no additional state of affairs can be instantiated in it without causing a contradiction.[4] So, Plantinga maintains that the free will defender is claiming that there is some describable maximal state of affairs in which it is true that both God and evil exist. Of course, to show this, the free will defender will suggest some possible proposition, e.g., it was not within God's power to create a world containing moral good but no moral evil,[5] that together with (A) entails (Z).

According to Plantinga, the opponent of the free will defense will maintain that (A) entails not (Z) but

(B) No free men God creates ever perform morally evil
actions.

The usual argument for the claim is this: That there be free men
who always freely do what is right is a possible state of affairs.
If God is omnipotent, he can bring about all possible states of
affairs. Given that God is good, he must bring about the state of
affairs that consists of free men always doing what is right.

Plantinga's response to this type of argument in his first
version of the free will defense was to maintain that there are
many possibilities God cannot bring about. In essence, this is
his tack in the revised version, but his argument is slightly
different. Instead of talking directly about God's omnipotence,
Plantinga talks about "Leibniz's Lapse," which is presupposed
in the argument against the free will defense. According to
Plantinga, Leibniz's lapse is Leibniz's mistaken claim that God
can instantiate any possible world in which he exists. This is a
mistake because there are some possible worlds God exists in
but cannot bring about. To show Leibniz's lapse, Plantinga
asks us to imagine a case of two men, Paul and the reader,
negotiating the purchase of an aardvark.[6] The reader offers Paul
$500 for the aardvark and is turned down. Knowing that the
going rate for aardvarks is $650, the reader wonders what Paul
would have done if he had been offered $700. Would he have
taken it or rejected it? Plantinga puts this question into the
following terms: Letting S' stand for the state of affairs that
includes the reader's offering Paul $700, Paul's being free to
accept or reject the money, the going rate being $650, and
everything else being as much as possible like the actual world,
the reader's question is equivalent to wondering which of the
following is true:

(23) If the state of affairs S' had obtained, Paul would have
accepted the offer.
(24) If the state of affairs S' had obtained, Paul would not
have accepted the offer.

It is clear that, since Paul is free, S''s obtaining does not entail
either that Paul accepts the offer or that he rejects it. That is,
there are possible worlds in which S' obtains and Paul rejects
the offer and possible worlds in which S' obtains and Paul
accepts the offer. Plantinga continues the argument:

> We are now in a position to grasp an important fact. Either
> (23) or (24) is in fact true; and either way there are pos-
> sible worlds God could not have actualized. Suppose,
> first of all, that (23) is true. Then it was beyond the
> power of God to create a world in which (1) Paul is free to
> sell his aardvark and free to refrain, and in which the
> other states of affairs included in S' obtain, and (2) Paul
> does not sell. That is, it was beyond his power to create a
> world in which ["S' obtains"] and ["Paul does not accept
> the offer"] are both true. There is at least one possible
> world like this, but God, despite His omnipotence, could
> not have brought about its actuality.[7]

This argument seems convincing. Given that (23) is in fact true,
God does not have the power to bring it about that S' obtain and
that Paul not accept the offer without taking away Paul's freedom.
Thus there is a possible world God cannot create, namely a
possible world in which (23) is true, S' obtains, and Paul does
not freely accept the offer. God cannot instantiate this possible
world because it would not be a consistently describable world.
For, given that (23) is true in a world and S' obtains in that
world, it logically follows that in that world Paul accepts the
offer. To add that in that world God brings it about that Paul
does not accept the offer is to create an inconsistent set, i.e., a
set that includes both Paul's accepting the offer and Paul's not
accepting the offer.
    Even if (23) is in fact true, it is important to note, however,
that there are possible worlds God could have created that
included S''s obtaining and Paul's not accepting the offer. Consider those possible worlds in which (24) is true.[8] In those
possible worlds, God has the power to bring about that Paul not
accept the offer by bringing it about that S' obtains. In all of
these possible worlds, if they are brought about by God, S'
would obtain and Paul would not accept the offer. I think it is
important to note that God could have instantiated such worlds
for this reason. Plantinga has shown that, given the truth in a
particular possible world of a certain conditional about how a
person would act in that world, there are certain events that
cannot obtain in that world and, consequently, possible worlds
God cannot bring about. But he has not shown that there are
not possible worlds in which God has the power to bring about
events ruled out in one possible world by the truth of a condi-

tional in that possible world. God, restrained by the truth of certain conditionals in one possible world, does not have the power to cause certain events to obtain in that world. He has the power, however, to cause the events to obtain in other possible worlds not restricted by the truth of those conditionals.

Of course, Plantinga may think that God is restrained by the truth of (23) in every possible world. If this is the case, God does not have the power to instantiate a world in which Paul does not accept the bribe, and there are, consequently, possible worlds God cannot bring about. But why would Plantinga maintain this? (23) and (24) are contingent propositions. According to the traditional understanding of omnipotence, the truth values of contingent propositions are subject to God's control. He chooses whether a sentence like (23) is true or false by his decision of what possible world to make actual. On this understanding of God's omnipotence, to maintain that God is restricted by the truth of sentences like (23) in the sense that he does not have the power to create states of affairs in which (23) is false is to deny God's omnipotence. Plantinga maintains that God is omnipotent. Perhaps he understands omnipotence in a way other than the traditional understanding. But if he does, one would expect some explicit justification of his departure from the traditional notion. Yet, in his treatments of omnipotence, the definition he offers is in line with the traditional notion of omnipotence as spelled out by, among others, Aquinas, Scotus, and Molina.[9] So Plantinga can maintain that God is restrained by the truth of sentences like (23) only by rejecting the traditional view of God's omnipotence, and it is uncertain that he wishes to do this.

Of course, sentences like (23) and (24) are a special type of contingent statements. They concern the actions of free, human agents. Forcing an agent like Paul to perform an action or to refrain from performing an action is not consistent with his libertarian freedom. Consequently, the existence of free actions do limit God's power in that it is not logically possible for God to force an agent to perform an action that is free in a libertarian sense. Given that (23) is in fact true, would God's bringing about worlds in which Paul refuses the offer violate Paul's freedom? Of course, if God were to bring about worlds in which (23) is true and in which Paul refuses the offer, we would think Paul's freedom was compromised. But if God brought about worlds in which (24) were true, why should we think that

Paul's freedom is compromised? In worlds in which (24) is true, Paul freely rejects the offer. There is no compromise of his freedom. Although I regard this line of reasoning as compelling, it might be regarded as too simple. One could argue (and I think Plantinga might) that the in fact truth of (23) means that Paul is so constituted that, no matter what the possible world is, so long as S' obtains, Paul would accept the offer. While Paul could have been other than he is, he is not; he will accept the offer whenever S' obtains.

In response to this reasoning, it is important to point out that one of the characteristics Plantinga specifies for S' is that it be otherwise just like the actual world (i.e., the world in which Paul freely accepts the bribe). That is, the conditions contained in S' must be exactly like the conditions obtaining in the actual world up to the point of the offer. Now it does seem reasonable to think that, if Paul freely behaves in a certain way under specified circumstances, he would behave the same way given the same specified circumstances. And if he did not, we would assume either that the same circumstances did not obtain or that Paul's freedom was interfered with. But if God is concerned with bringing about a world in which Paul rejects the offer, why would he bring about circumstances in which Paul would freely accept the offer? Should he not bring about a possible world different from the actual world in which, for example, there are strong inducements not to sell little animals? In such a world, albeit with conditions different from those obtaining in the actual world, Paul would freely reject the offer. And if God were omnipotent, he should be able to bring about worlds with these contingent conditions. To maintain otherwise would compromise his omnipotence. Thus it appears that God could bring it about that Paul freely reject the offer. He could do so either by bringing about worlds in which (24) is true or by bringing about worlds in which contingent conditions lead Paul to reject the offer freely. To deny that he can so act appears to be in conflict with God's omnipotence as traditionally understood.

Plantinga's purpose in discussing the aardvark story is to save the free will defense by showing that there are possible worlds God cannot bring about. Showing this is not sufficient to save the defense, however. For, to do this Plantinga must show that it is possible that among the worlds God cannot bring about are the worlds in which free persons always freely do what is right.

Plantinga is aware of this and addresses the problem through another story.

Plantinga imagines a story about a fictional mayor of Boston, Curley Smith, and a highway proposed by L. B. Smedes, the director of highways.[10] Curley Smith opposes construction of the highway, but is bribed by Smedes to drop his opposition for $35,000. Smedes then wonders if he could have bribed Curley Smith for $20,000. To Plantinga, in pondering this, Smedes is pondering the truth of

(31) If Smedes had offered Curley a bribe of $20,000, he would have accepted it.

Plantinga then asks us to imagine a state of affairs, S', which he calls a "maximal world segment," that has these characteristics: (1) it includes Curley's being offered a bribe of $20,000; (2) it does not include either his accepting the bribe or rejecting it; (3) it is otherwise as much as possible like the actual world; (4) it is such that adding to it any state of affairs compatible with it but not included in it will result in an entire possible world. Plantinga then asks us to imagine that (31) is true. So we add a fifth characteristic to S', i.e., (5) it is such that if it were actual, Curley would have accepted the bribe. Plantinga numbers this fifth condition (32) for purposes of his discussion.

Having specified all this, Plantinga maintains:

> Now, of course, there is at least one possible world, W', in which S' is actual and Curley does not take the bribe. But God could not have created W'; to do so, He would have been obliged to actualize S', leaving Curley free with respect to the action of taking the bribe. But under these conditions Curley, as (32) [i.e., if S' were actual, Curley would have accepted the bribe] assures us, would have accepted the bribe, so that the world thus created would not have been W'.

So far, this story is very similar to the aardvark story discussed above. In the aardvark story, Plantinga demonstrated that, given the truth in a possible world (our actual world) of a certain conditional about Paul's behavior, there are events God is not able to bring about. Likewise, in the Curley case, given the truth of (32) in a possible world, God is not able to bring it about in that world that S' obtains and that Curley does not accept the bribe. Moreover, if we allow that (32) is true in our actual world, we would even say that God is not able to bring it about in the actual world that S' obtains and that Curley not accept the bribe. But none of this shows that God could not have created a possible world with other circumstances in which Curley rejects the bribe. Nor does it show that God could not have, in some possible world, brought it about that S' obtains and that Curley does not accept the bribe. For consider the possible world W^g in which it is true that, if Smedes had offered Curley a bribe of $20,000, he would not have accepted. In this possible world, we can describe a maximal world segment, S', having the characteristics Plantinga specifies in his Curley story with the exception of the fifth characteristic. Instead of imagining that, if S' were actual, Curley would have accepted the bribe [Plantinga's (32)], we imagine that in W^g this is true:

(33) If S' were actual, Curley would not have accepted the bribe.

God is able to bring it about in the possible world W^g that S' obtains and that Curley does not accept the bribe. Of course, if we desire a world in which all persons always freely do what is right, we would wonder why God did not instantiate the possible world W^g rather than the world in which (32) is true. The fact that he could have, but did not, counts against the free will defense.[11]

Plantinga, perhaps, has this objection in mind, for he continues with the Curley case.

> Curley, as we see, is not above a bit of Watergating. But there may be worse to come. Of course, there are possible worlds in which he is significantly free (i.e., free with respect to a morally significant action) and never does what is wrong. But the sad truth about Curley may be this. Consider W', any of these worlds: in W' Curley is significantly free, so in W' there are some actions that are morally significant for him and with respect to which he is free. But at least one of these actions—call it A—has the following peculiar property. There is a maximal world segment S' that obtains in W' and is such that (1) S' includes Curley's being free re A but neither his perform-

ing A nor his refraining from A; (2) S' is otherwise as much as possible like W'; and (3) if S' had been actual, Curley would have gone wrong with respect to A. (Notice that this third condition holds, in fact, in the actual world; it does not hold in that world W'.)

Plantinga claims that this passage indicates that God could not have actualized W'. But since W' is any of the worlds in which Curley is significantly free but always does only what is right, it follows that the passage shows that God could not have created a world in which Curley produces moral good but no moral evil, for "[e]very world God can actualize is such that if Curley is significantly free in it, he takes at least one wrong action."[12] Plantinga further explains that in his story Curley suffers from a malady called "transworld depravity" and gives this explicit definition of it:

A person P suffers from transworld depravity if and only if the following holds: for every world W such that P is significantly free in W and P does only what is right in W, there is an action A and a maximal world segment S' such that

(1) S' includes A's being morally significant for P
(2) S' includes P's being free with respect to A
(3) S' is included in W and includes neither P's performing A nor P's refraining from performing A.
(4) If S' were actual, P would go wrong with respect to A. (In thinking about this definition, remember that (4) is to be true in fact in the actual world—not in the world W.)

Having stated this definition, Plantinga emphasizes that the importance "about the idea of transworld depravity is that if a person suffers from it, then it wasn't within God's power to actualize any world in which that person is significantly free but does no wrong—that is, a world in which he produces moral good but no moral evil."[13] So, presumably, Plantinga has now answered the question posed above: Why did not God instantiate one of those possible worlds in which Curley would not accept the bribe? His answer is that since it is possible that Curley suffers from transworld depravity, it is possible that

God did not have the power to instantiate any of the possible worlds in which Curley would not accept the bribe. But is Plantinga justified in claiming this?

In his explicit definition of transworld depravity, Plantinga cautions: "in thinking about this definition, remember that (4) is to be true in fact, in the actual world—not in that world W." This qualification is difficult to understand. Plantinga makes it because he does not want to claim that there are no possible worlds in which a person (in this case Curley) is significantly free and always does what is right. He thus wants to allow that there are possible worlds, W, in which a person always does what is right. He captures this desire by saying that (4) is true in the actual world but not in the world W. But, if (4) is true in the actual world (our world), then it follows that in the actual world (our world), if S' obtains, God does not have the power to make P (in this case Curley) not go wrong in the actual world with respect to A. Thus, the possible world constituted by the truth of (4) and the obtaining of S' could not be a possible world W in which P always does only what is right.

Yet, we may still wonder why it is that, given the truth of (4) in our actual world, God would have chosen to actualize our actual world rather than some other possible world in which (4) is not true. For if, in some possible world, (4) is not true and in that possible world it is true that, if S' were actual, P would not go wrong with respect to A, God has the power to have brought it about that P would not go wrong with respect to A. He could have done this merely by instantiating S'.

In response to this question, I do not think Plantinga can maintain that there are no possible worlds in which (4) is false. Plantinga himself maintains that S' is included in at least one world W in which Curley takes the bribe and in at least one world W' in which he rejects it.[14] And one can express this claim by saying that in W (4) is true and in W' (4) is false. Nor do I think that Plantinga can merely maintain that, although there are possible worlds in which (4) is false, God does not have the power to bring these about. While it is true that God, having instantiated our actual world and having subjected himself to the restrictions of our actual world, does not have the power to bring about W', God could have brought about W' instead of W. And the central question being posed against Plantinga is why God did not do other than he did. To say that he could not do other than act in accordance with the truth of the contingent conditional (4) is to embrace a very untraditional notion of God's omnipotence—one that requires some explicit defense. Moreover, we still have the question I have repeatedly raised: If God wants Curley always to do freely what is right, why did God not create a world whose circumstances would lead to Curley's freely rejecting the bribe? The conditions of this world leading up to Curley's being offered the bribe would not match the conditions contained in S', of course, but this hardly seems to matter if we are wondering why there is not a world without evil.

Thus, I cannot see how Plantinga's notion of a person's suffering from transworld depravity answers the questions posed against the free will defense: Why did not God instantiate a possible world (different from our actual world) in which persons always freely do what is right? But Plantinga has not yet finished with the Curley story.

Plantinga points out that someone might offer the following objection to his notion of transworld depravity:

> For suppose all the people that exist in Kronos, the actual world, suffer from transworld depravity; it doesn't follow that God could not have created a world containing moral good without creating one containing moral evil. God could have created other people. Instead of creating us, i.e., the people that exist in Kronos, He could have created a world containing people, but not containing any of us—or perhaps a world containing some of us along with some others who do not exist in Kronos. And perhaps if He'd done that, He could have created a world containing moral good but no moral evil.[15]

In order to answer this objection, Plantinga says we must think about "individual natures" or "essences." Basically, an essence of a person is the set of properties that are essential to him, i.e., the properties he has in every possible world in which he exists. Among the properties a person has as part of his essence are world-indexed properties. These are the properties a person has in any specific world, e.g., being snub-nosed in the actual world, being aquiline-nosed in possible world W', and so on.[16] Every person is, for Plantinga, an instantiation of some essence. In particular, Curley Smith is the instantiation of the essence of Curley Smith. Let us now return to Plantinga's argument:

> Returning to Curley, we recall that he suffers from transworld depravity. This fact implies something interesting about Curleyhood, Curley's essence. Take those worlds W such that "is significantly free in W" and "never does what is wrong in W" are contained in Curley's essence. Each of these worlds has an important property if Curley suffers from transworld depravity; each is such that God could not have created or actualized it.[17]

In order to demonstrate his claim that, if Curley suffers from transworld depravity, God could not have actualized any possible world in which Curley never does what is wrong, Plantinga refers us back to his discussion of transworld depravity. He once again gives an argument about certain characteristics of a maximal state of affairs S', the truth of a conditional about S', and a morally significant action A. According to Plantinga this argument shows that God could not have created any world W such that Curleyhood contains the properties "is significantly free in W" and "always does what is right."[18]

Having claimed this about Curleyhood, Plantinga talks more generally about essences and transworld depravity. After indicating that "if E is a person's essence, then that person is the instantiation of E" and that "to instantiate an essence, God creates a person who has the essence" Plantinga defines an essence's suffering from transworld depravity in this way:

> An essence E suffers from transworld depravity if and only if for every world W such that E contains the properties "is significantly free in W" and "always does what is right in W," there is an action A and a maximal world segment S' such that
>
> (1) S' includes E's being instantiated and E's instantiation being free with respect to A and A's being morally significant for E's instantiation.
> (2) S' is included in W but includes neither E's instantiation performing A nor E's instantiation's refraining from A.
> (3) If S' were actual, then the instantiation of E would have gone wrong with respect to A.[19]

According to Plantinga, if an essence E suffers from transworld depravity, then it was not within God's power to actualize a possible world W such that E contains the properties "is significantly free in W" and "always does what is right in W." Thus, according to Plantinga, it is possible that every essence including the property of being created by God suffers from transworld depravity. If this is true, then God could not have created a world containing moral good but no moral evil. And, if this is true, of course, the free will defense is triumphant. God did create a world containing creatures who perform moral evil; but there is nothing else he could have done given that he instantiated a world containing creatures. Thus, it would seem that the possibility that all creaturely essences suffer from transworld depravity vindicates the free will defense. Or does it? In order to answer this question, we must return to Plantinga's definition of what it is for an essence to suffer from transworld depravity.

The problematic clause of the definition is the third condition. In the explicit definition that Plantinga gives for a person's suffering from transworld depravity, he remarked that the conditional "if S′ had been actual, Curley would have gone wrong with respect to A" is true in the actual world. In the definition of the transworld depravity of essences, there is no such qualification.[20] I do not know whether this is an oversight on Plantinga's part or if the exclusion is intentional. If it is an oversight, the considerations I have already offered against earlier versions of transworld depravity would also argue against this version.

But perhaps Plantinga purposefully refrained from qualifying clause (3) with the claim that it is true in fact in the actual world but not in that possible world W. If so, then clause (3) is meant to state one of two things. On the one hand, it might mean that in any possible world, if S′ were actual in that world, then the instantiation of E in that possible world would have gone wrong in the world with respect to A. But this cannot be the intended reading of clause (3). This reading would rule out the logical possibility of an instantiation of E going right with respect to A.

On the other hand, clause (3) might mean that in any possible world *in which God made* S′ actual, the instantiation of E would have gone wrong in that world with respect to A. This does seem like the intended reading of clause (3), for this reading allows that there are possible worlds in which the instantiation of E does not go wrong with respect to A but also indicates that it was not in God's power to instantiate these worlds. But if this is the intended reading of clause (3), why should we accept it as possibly true? Given that there are possible worlds in which an instantiation of E goes right with respect to A, why should we think it is possible that it was not in God's power to instantiate them?

In his most recent reply to Plantinga, Pike discusses the nature of God's activity in making possible worlds actual.[21] If we refrain from employing the details of Pike's story and stay with the terminology of possible worlds, essences, and instantiations of essences, Pike's remarks may be stated in this way. God does not constitute essences. Since they are consistent sets of certain properties, they exist independent of God's activity. And what the instantiation of an essence would do in a possible world is also independent of God's action.[22] All that God does is choose which instantiation of an essence actually exists in the world he actualizes. The actions of that instantiation of the essence are, of course, in accord with the nature of the instantiation that is independent of God's actions. If God can, as Plantinga admits, instantiate in some possible world an essence that would go wrong relative to an action A in that possible world and God can do so without compromising the freedom of the instantiation of the essence, why can God not instantiate an essence in some possible world that would not go wrong relative to the action A in that possible world? Since Plantinga admits that there are possible worlds in which an instantiation of an essence goes right with respect to A and God's creative activity is limited to allowing instantiations of essences to exist in possible worlds, why did he not instantiate the essence in the possible world in which the instantiation goes right relative to A? To maintain that God, as he exists in our actual world subject to conditionals true in our actual world, did not have the power to do this is not a sufficient reply for Plantinga. He must show why this very untraditional conception of God's omnipotence should be accepted. Without this explanation, one must think that his version of the free will defense fails.

There is an even more serious problem if we read clause (3) as the claim that it is possible that in any possible world *in which God made S′* actual, the instantiation of E would have gone wrong in that world with respect to A. Recall that Plantinga has stated that the free will defense rests on demonstrating that it is possible that

(30) God is omnipotent, and it was not within His power to create a world containing moral good but no moral evil.[23]

Plantinga's notion of an essence's suffering from transworld depravity is part of the demonstration that (30) is possible. Indeed, Plantinga argues that (30) is possible by stating that it is possible that all creaturely essences suffer from transworld depravity. As we have seen, the claim that it is possible that all creaturely essences are so afflicted rests on the claim that the third clause of the definition of an essence's suffering from transworld depravity is possible. And if we read (3) as the claim that it is possible that in any possible world *in which God made* S' actual, the instantiation of E would have gone wrong in that world with respect to A, we would be saying that the proof of the possibility of (30) rests on the claim that it is possible that in any possible world *in which God made* S' actual, the instantiation of E would have gone wrong in that world with respect to A. This latter claim, however, seems to be an *explanation* of how it is possible that God cannot create a world containing moral good but no moral evil; that is, if it is possible that in whatever world God brings about there is a maximal world segment S' and an action A such that the instantiation of E would go wrong in that world with respect to A, then it is indeed possible that God does not have the power to create a world containing moral good but no moral evil. But an explanation is not an argument. Before we would be willing to accept that the intended reading of clause (3) justifies the possibility of (30), we would surely demand some argument that the intended reading of clause (3) is possible. But how could someone show that clause (3) under the intended reading is possible? It certainly is not prima facie possible. For if we withdraw from Plantinga's technical formulation of the free will defense, the following facts emerge. Most people would assume that God could have brought it about that there is a world in which all creatures freely do right—unless arguments to the contrary are presented. Indeed, Plantinga recognizes this and tries to argue against this assumption. But if God could have brought it about that there is a world in which all creatures freely do what is right, it follows that, in some possible world God could have brought about, the instantiations of the relevant essences would have always freely done what is right. And this would be accepted by most people concerned with the free will debate. To offer as an argument against this that it is possible that, in all the possible worlds God could bring about, the instantiations of the relevant essences would have gone wrong is not an argument at all. It is merely a denial of what must be argued against. In short, Plantinga has not really discharged his obligation to demonstrate the possibility of (30). It seems that despite all the technical apparatus he employs, Plantinga has not vindicated the free will defense.

PIKE'S REFORMULATION OF THE FREE WILL DEFENSE

In his most recent contribution to the Pike–Plantinga exchange on the free will defense,[24] Pike has offered a broad review of what the defense should be. His discussion begins with an assessment of Robert Adams's remarks about middle knowledge.[25]

On Pike's interpretation, Adams can be understood as both attacking and supporting Plantinga's version of the free will defense. On the negative side, Adams claims that Plantinga is surely wrong to endorse middle knowledge. The doctrine, understood as the claim that God can know what free creatures *would* do in any circumstances, is incoherent. At best, according to Adams, God could only know what creatures *would probably* do in various circumstances. But this negative point against Plantinga also suggests a positive point in Plantinga's favor: God might not be able to guarantee that men always freely do what is right. On the new understanding of middle knowledge, God might create creatures he thinks would probably always do what is right. Unfortunately, given the nature of probability, it turns out that the creatures he creates perform a great amount of evil. Of course, God is not to blame for this because he does the best he can, given that only what creatures would probably do can be known. Thus God might create a world full of evil and be justified in this creation. Pike, however, thinks there are difficulties even with this version of the defense.

In considering this Adamsesque reformulation of Plantinga's argument, Pike appeals to our notions about responsible action:

> Having dispensed with dispositional choice properties of the 'would' variety, we are back to a position mentioned in the second section of this paper, viz., prior to the act of creation, God could know only that the world to be actualized would *probably* contain a balance of morally right actions over morally wrong actions. When one considers

the immense amount of suffering and sorrow that has already been exacted as the grim down payment, it is not at all clear that a fully responsible creator would risk the investment given something less than complete assurance of success.[26]

Pike is, in effect, claiming that, were God to create on the basis of probabilities, we must question his moral goodness. But, in response to Pike, a staunch free will defender could claim that the creation of free creatures is so valuable as to outweigh any of the evils coming from free will and so God would be morally justified in creating a world full of freely performed evil.[27] Such a line of reasoning would refute Pike's claim because such a defender already grants that good outweighs evil by the mere fact that God created free creatures. Should such a free will defender even endorse the new version of Plantinga's argument? I think not, for there is a difficulty with the Adamsesque reformulation.

Adams's discussion of middle knowledge centers around what God could know about the future actions of the citizens of Keilah if David hid from Saul in their town. Adams claims that God could only know that the citizens would probably give up David if Saul beseiged the town. This is so because God could know what they would freely do only by knowing their intentions and character traits, and people can act contrary to intentions and out of character. But there is something very odd about this. God would know how people would probably act only, presumably, by observing how people in fact act in various circumstances.[28] But this implies that there are people who exist and who can be observed. And this spells disaster for the probabilistic version of middle knowledge. For, in order for God to have the type of knowledge (of traits, intentions, and so on) required for middle knowledge so that he could create people who would probably do good, he must already have created people. And there would be no guarantee about how these people would probably act. So, when God creates the universe and decides, for example, what sort of Adam and Eve to create, he must make judgments about what sort of couple to make in the absence of data on what actual persons do in various circumstances. Indeed, his choice to create certain persons is what makes persons actual. Thus middle knowledge formulated as a probabilistic doctrine (in a Humean sense) is no aid to God in choosing what creatures to make actual. He can have probabilistic knowledge only if there are actual creatures, and by then it could be too late for God to prevent the consequences of his original choice of creatures. If we grant that God cannot significantly interfere with the free actions of creatures, then once the Adam and Eve he chooses to create exist, he cannot significantly interfere with their decisions about how to live their lives, when to produce offspring, how to raise children, and so on.[29] In effect, in terms of the moral actions of creatures, God's first choice about whom to make is his last. Once those beings exist, he can persuade, cajole, and establish favorable or unfavorable conditions for actions, but this is all he can do if he does not significantly interfere with the free actions of creatures. But perhaps God should significantly interfere with the free actions of creatures. This leads us to the second part of Pike's overview.

Pike indicates that Plantinga, throughout his treatment of the free will defense, has failed to distinguish God's being unable to create creatures that always do right from God's being able to create creatures that never do what is wrong.[30] This is a mistake, for, according to Pike, even if it is possible that God cannot do the former, he can still bring about the latter by causing potential wrongdoers to refrain from the performance of immoral actions. While I agree with Pike that there is a distinction between the two situations, it is not at all clear that God could cause potential wrongdoers to refrain from immoral actions without violating a libertarian sense of freedom. To simplify my argument for this claim, let us focus on one evil action: Larry Moe's shooting of Curley Joe.

Assume that after years of working together, Larry Moe has formed a hatred of Curley Joe, and decides to do away with him by shooting him in a back alley. By devious means, Larry Moe lures Curley Joe into an alley, pulls out a hand gun, and shoots him. How could God prevent the performance of this immoral action?

There seem to be two possible ways. God could intervene by influencing Larry Moe's hatred of Curley Joe and by changing Larry Moe's resolve to kill Curley Joe. But I think that this would surely be in violation of a libertarian sense of freedom, since Larry Moe is not acting in accordance with his real desires.

On the other hand, God could cause the gun to misfire, or the bullet to go astray, or the Bible Curley Joe always carries to shield off the bullet, and so on. Such intervention would not obviously conflict with the freedom of Larry Moe's actions. God could, of course, act in a similar way on every occasion of a potentially evil act. So, apparently, God could prevent much of the effects of moral evil without eliminating freedom. So why does he not do it?

While in this latter case it is more difficult to see a compromise of freedom, I think ultimately there is a violation of a libertarian sense of freedom. If every time (or a significant number of times) someone tried to cause evil the action went awry, surely human beings would conclude that there is someone or something interfering with their actions. They would think, undoubtedly, that they were not free to perform evil actions because, although they had the ability to cause evil, they had not the opportunity to exercise the ability because someone or something was preventing the evil effects. Perhaps Pike has some other scenario in mind, but failing a specification of such a scenario, I cannot think of a way God could guarantee that there be no persons who do evil—given that he creates people who will not freely do right always.

LESSONS LEARNED

Having examined Plantinga's free will defense and its possible variations, Pike in his most recent article strikes out into new ground with his exchange with Plantinga. He begins his remarks with an historical observation. According to Pike, Plantinga's version of the free will defense is very different from the defense offered by Augustine. On Pike's understanding, Augustine believes that God can know what men would freely do. Moreover, Augustine holds that God can create men who always freely do what is right as well as men who sometimes do what is evil. God, however, chooses to create men who would freely do evil because in some mysterious way, known only to God, creation of these men contributes more toward an ultimate good than does the creation of men who always freely do what is right. To hearken back to an article Pike wrote many years ago,[31] Pike is arguing that Augustine's free will defense is really an argument that, although God could have made a world containing only persons who always freely do what is right, he did not but is not morally blameworthy for this because he has a morally sufficient reason for his action. Thus, if Plantinga is trying to offer a defense in the spirit of Augustine, he should not rest his argument on the possibility that it is not in God's power to create persons who always freely do what is right.

Pike's remarks are intriguing. Oddly enough, they seem to indicate that Augustine did not intend to offer a free will defense. For the fact that people freely perform the actions they do is not essential to his position. But what is striking about Pike's discussion is his attempt to ground Plantinga's remarks in historical figures. I think there are historical sources other than Augustine for many of the issues brought up in the Pike–Plantinga exchange on the free will defense and that these should also receive attention.

It is interesting to note that the Plantinga–Pike exchange is built on the assumption that God's omniscience extends to the future, free actions of human beings. In order to explain this knowledge, Plantinga endorsed what appears to be Molina's doctrine of middle knowledge. As we have seen, the doctrine is full of difficulties. Since Pike throughout the stages of the debate is conceding to Plantinga as much as he can in order to defeat Plantinga's argument, he also grants that God can know the future, free actions of persons. Pike's explanation of God's knowledge is, however, different from Plantinga's. Throughout the debate, Pike seems to endorse something like a Leibnizian-Scotistic explanation.[32] Pike assumes that the possible persons God can instantiate have properties like "if instantiated would make a right turn at Campus and University Streets on April 19, 1986." Because the possible persons have these properties and God knows the make-up of possible persons, he knows what future, free actions persons would perform. This, in fact, appears to be a plausible explanation of God's knowledge of these future, free acts. Yet, there is a question that can be raised against this explanation: If possible persons have such properties, are they free in a libertarian sense? This is an important question for Pike because he seems to endorse a libertarian notion of freedom. Unfortunately, given Pike's comments on possible persons, the question must be answered in the negative. A possible person on Pike's view is simply identical to the sum of the properties it has. If some person p were to have properties different from the set it has, it would be a possible person different from the person p. In short, all the properties of a possible person on Pike's view are essential to it. It cannot have different properties and retain its identity. But if this is so, a possible person cannot be free in a libertarian sense. It must act in accordance with the properties it has. Of course, we have seen this before; it is merely a restatement of Arnauld's objection to article 13 of Leibniz's *Discourse on Metaphysics*.[33] As Leibniz realized, the objection can be answered only by adopting a non-libertarian view of freedom. Similarly, the objection shows that Pike cannot think that God knows the future actions of creatures by seeing the properties creatures have and maintain a libertarian notion of freedom.

Yet, if we do not embrace Pike's (and Scotus' and Leibniz's) view of how God knows the future actions of creatures, we have no explanation of God's knowledge. To say that possible persons are sets of alternative properties, i.e., properties like "can turn right at Campus and University or can turn left," seems to preserve a libertarian sense of freedom but provides no explanation of how God knows what action a person will take. We have seen that middle knowledge provides no explanation of God's knowledge, and so we cannot appeal to that doctrine. Appeal to probabilistic explanation also fails. Moreover, the purely intellectualistic explanation that all is present to God falls prey to the difficulties Scotus and Molina pointed out. And to claim that somehow God knows the future, free actions of creatures is, of course, no explanation at all.

It thus appears that our investigation of Scotus and his intellectual descendants has left us with an important lesson. Those who are in the Christian tradition face a difficult choice; either they say that God's omniscience extends to the future, free actions of men and give up a libertarian notion of freedom, or they say that men are free in a libertarian sense and claim that God does not know the future, free actions of men. The choice is difficult because each alternative seems to run afoul of basic Christian beliefs. To deny freedom in a libertarian sense seems tantamount to rejecting the basis of Christian morality. On the other hand, to deny that God knows the future, free actions of men seems to compromise his omniscience—unless one denies that future, free actions are in principle knowable. Since omniscience is, roughly speaking, knowing all that is knowable, if future, free actions are not knowable, God could be omniscient and not know future, free actions. In fact, some people have endorsed this position.[34] It does not sit well with the Christian tradition, however, for most in the tradition think that God's omniscience does encompass future, free actions.

Thus the difficult choice for Christians appears to be a dilemma.

Yet, there is an alternative to the dilemma: a rejection of a libertarian notion of freedom in favor of a compatibilist notion. If this alternative is accepted, both human freedom and God's omniscience in the strong sense can be salvaged. Indeed, as we have seen, many important figures in the Christian tradition — Calvin, Luther, Leibniz — have endorsed this option.

It is important to note, however, that if this option is taken, Pike's comments about the Augustinian "free will" defense become extremely important. Given a compatibilist definition of 'freedom', God could create a world in which all persons freely do what is right. It is clear that he does not, however. Why not? As Pike's Augustine said, God must have a morally sufficient reason for doing so; for example, perhaps in some "unspeakably strange and wonderful way" the creation of the sometimes evil people we see contributes more to an ultimate good than does the creation of people who always do what is right.

Plantinga's technical refinement of the free will defense is unsuccessful. Despite this failure, Plantinga's discussion of the defense and the subsequent Pike–Plantinga exchange have revealed a number of important considerations about freedom, omniscience, God's creative activity, and so on. It is interesting that many of the points both Pike and Plantinga make about these issues were discussed by earlier thinkers like Molina and Leibniz. As I have argued in previous chapters, many of these issues grew out of the formulations of Duns Scotus. In the next chapter, I wish to apply what has emerged from the discussions of the last three chapters to the doctrines of Duns Scotus.

Part III
A Re-examination of
Scotus' Doctrine

7 Scotus' Theory of God's Omniscience in Retrospect

In the preceding chapters, I have explained Scotus' theory of God's omniscience and the theories of his intellectual successors. It is clear that Scotus' theory is important both philosophically and historically. Not only does he present an intriguing analysis of God's knowledge, but what is more, many of the significant discussions of God's omniscience have grown out of his problematic. In the present chapter, I wish to return once more to Scotus' theory and employ the insights gained from examining Scotus' descendants to summarize and examine that theory.

Scotus' explanation of God's omniscience was formulated for two different but related reasons. In the first place, in examining his predecessors' theories, especially that of Aquinas, Scotus discovered what he took to be two important flaws: Aquinas' emphasis on the presentiality of certain contingents to the eternal now collapses the differences among past, present, and future; and Aquinas' analysis fails to acknowledge sufficiently the role God's will must play in his knowledge. In the second place, as a voluntarist, Scotus wanted to stress the dominance of God's will over his intellect. He particularly wanted to emphasize that God's will is important for even the primary activity of God's intellect: knowing.

As we have seen, it is not at all clear that Aquinas' analysis of omniscience entails a collapse of present, past, and future. Successors of Aquinas, especially Cajetan and Molina, attempted to neutralize the difficulty by distinguishing a temporal from an eternal sense of 'now'. Such a distinction, they argued, cuts through the ambiguities of Aquinas' analysis of omniscience and renders the doctrine coherent.

Scotus' second criticism, however, is less easily disposed of. Indeed, much of the discussion about God's omniscience after Scotus and Aquinas centered around this very issue: What are the relationships among possibilities, God's willing activity, and his knowledge of actualities? Scotus claimed that, without God's willing activity, God could know only mere possibilities. Simply put, unless God wills possibilities to be actual, there are no actualities. Thus God's knowledge of actualities must be related to his willing activity.

Even Aquinas was aware that God must will certain possibilities to be actual; according to Scotus' reading of Aquinas, God must directly will non-voluntary states of affairs into existence. God cannot, however, directly will the voluntary actions of free agents into existence without compromising their freedom. Aquinas therefore proposed a two-part theory of God's knowledge of contingents: God knows non-voluntary contingents through his causality, and he knows the contingent acts of voluntary agents by those acts being present in their actuality to his eternity.

Scotus saw serious difficulties in Aquinas' claims about the presentiality of the acts of voluntary agents. Their acts are present to God's eternity only by being performed by actual agents. But these agents are actual only by being instantiated by God. And God must instantiate them as agents with complete lifestories, i.e., as agents who perform certain actions. To claim that God can only know the actions of agents as these actions are performed is, according to Scotus, to deny God's omniscience; for it is to deny that God can know all the possible actions of free agents. Therefore, according to Scotus, even the actions of voluntary agents must be subject to God's willing activity.

It is interesting that Molina saw similar problems in Aquinas' analysis. According to Molina, on Aquinas' analysis, there are many possibilities God cannot know if he knows voluntary actions only as present to him. For example, he could not know what some possible, but unactualized, free person would do in some circumstances since the unactualized person does not perform actual actions. Nor could God know what any actual person would do in any circumstances other than those that in fact obtained. He could not know this because these actions are never actual and therefore can never be present to the eternal now. Molina's objections are real difficulties for Aquinas' analysis. Clearly, the possible actions of possible persons as well as the possible actions of actual persons are possibilities an omniscient being should know. Yet, on Aquinas' analysis, these possibilities cannot be known by God, and so God appears not to be omniscient.

Scotus' own analysis of omniscience—that God knows all possibilities through his intellect alone and actualities by his willing certain possibilities to be actual—does not compromise God's omniscience. Given Scotus' analysis, God knows all past, present, and future contingent states of affairs—whether possible or actual. Yet, the price paid for this knowledge seems to be a loss of freedom: Human beings cannot do other than God wills and hence seem not to be free. As we have seen, Molina rejected Scotus' theory because of this difficulty. Yet, Molina's criticism was misguided, for Scotus does not endorse Molina's libertarian notion of freedom. On the contrary, given God's omniscience, Scotus holds that men are free only in a non-libertarian sense.

Scotus came to this conclusion because he claimed that every sufficient analysis of God's omniscience as it is traditionally understood must involve God's willing activity. There is much wisdom in Scotus' assessment. The Thomistic analysis obviously requires God's willing activity, as does Molina's doctrine of middle knowledge. Leibniz's virtually wholesale agreement with Scotus, and Plantinga's and Pike's insistence that God instantiates possible persons further strengthen Scotus' claim.

But once God's willing activity is made part of his omniscience, there is an obvious conflict with human freedom. Scotus saw the only possible resolution of this conflict in a rejection of a libertarian sense of 'freedom'. There is wisdom in this rejection as well. Given the need for God's willing activity, a purely intellectualistic analysis of omniscience joined to a libertarian view of freedom will not succeed. Moreover, the position of

Molina and Plantinga that omniscience and libertarianism can be rescued through middle knowledge is unsuccessful, for middle knowledge compromises a libertarian notion of freedom. Despite the wisdom in Scotus' rejection of libertarianism, however, there is an oversight in his analysis of omniscience—one that Leibniz saw.

Both Scotus and Leibniz understood that God could know what agents would do only if the future actions of agents were somehow part of the agent at all times of the agent's life. Although Scotus did not explain in great detail how the future actions are part of the agent, he would probably have found Leibniz's notion of complete, individual concepts an adequate explanation. Of course, once these concepts are accepted as part of the explanation of God's knowledge of future actions, one can only conclude that free agents are determined. This determination would not, however, be the result of God's activity. As Leibniz saw, and as Scotus failed to see, God only wills into existence what is, logically speaking, available to him, and he in no way changes what he wills into existence. The beings he makes actual are determined by virtue of the complete, individual concepts connected with them and not by his activity. Given this determinism, both Scotus and Leibniz could only opt for a non-libertarian notion of freedom to preserve the freedom of free agents.

Scotus' non-libertarian notion of freedom is complex. According to Scotus, an agent is free as regards some action x if and only if (1) the agent has the ability to perform x and the ability to refrain from performing x, and (2) the agent wills the performance (or the refraining from the performing) of x in accordance with his nature. It is clear that this definition of 'freedom' is related to what becomes known after Scotus' time as the liberty of spontaneity: An agent is free if it acts in accordance with its wishes without external compulsion. Moreover, it is clear that Scotus' definition rests on his interesting views about the abilities of agents.

As I have shown in the first part of this essay, implicit in Scotus' view of abilities is a distinction between an ability and the exercise of an ability. According to Scotus, an agent may have an ability even if he never has an opportunity to exercise it. Thus, when Scotus maintains that the possession of the ability to perform an action and the ability to refrain from performing the action is a necessary condition of freedom, he is not endorsing a libertarian notion of freedom. Obviously, there are difficulties in establishing that an agent possesses an ability that he never exercises, but the difficulties are not insurmountable. For example, we can appeal to the exercise of certain abilities that an agent possesses in order to establish that the agent has a similar ability he does not exercise. A case in point is when we say that someone who climbs mountains has the ability to climb the stairs in the Empire State Building. Presumably, if the ability in question is not too specific, e.g., the ability to hit a glass-shattering high note, we can even establish abilities by appealing to the actions other human beings perform. For example, to determine whether a seemingly normal human being named "Paul" can walk across a street, we can appeal to the fact that other normal human beings cross it daily.

Scotus' non-libertarian definition is also closely connected with his views about what we would call in a more contemporary vocabulary "possible persons." In effect, Scotus, along with Leibniz, holds that each person can be found in only one possible world. All of the properties of an individual are therefore essential to his identity; consequently, all the actions a possible person performs must be performed in order for the being to be himself. A libertarian analysis of freedom, such as the analysis urged by Molina, requires that possible persons be found in more than one possible world. If a person can do other than he does, as the libertarian claims, he must exist not only in the possible world in which he performs the action but also in the possible world defined by the alternative action. As it turns out, while Scotus' views about possible persons are essential to his discussion of how God knows what people freely do, these views compromise his analysis.

The first difficulty, as many have pointed out, is a difficulty for Leibniz as well.[1] Scotus believes that some of the properties of an individual are accidental while others are essential. For example, the property of being a man is essential to Socrates, but the property of having a beard is only accidental, for Socrates would be Socrates even without a beard. Yet, if Scotus maintains that the properties of an individual constitute the identity of the individual, it is difficult to see how he can say that some of a creature's properties are only accidental. If, for example, Socrates' property of having a beard is part of his identity, then he could not be Socrates unless he had a beard; thus, having a beard would be an essential property of Socrates even though intuitively we would judge that it is only an accidental property.

Scotus could set about solving this difficulty by claiming that some properties can be accidental to a creature and yet be essential to its identity. He could do this by distinguishing "having a property" from "having a property at a certain time." Consider the case of Socrates who grows a beard when he is twenty and shaves it off when he is forty. It is clear that, on Scotus' theory of possible persons, for Socrates to be Socrates he must have a beard from the age of twenty to the age of thirty-nine. Having the beard during these years is essential to his identity. Not having a beard at the age of forty is likewise essential to Socrates' identity. But if we consider the property of having a beard, it is clear that this property is not essential to Socrates, for he has a beard from the age of twenty to the age of thirty-nine and he does not have one at forty. Thus, while having a beard may be an accidental property of Socrates, it is necessary to his identity that he have (or lack) a beard at different times. Similar arguments can be made for many of Socrates' properties, e.g., having a snub nose, having a deep tan, and so on. In general, on Scotus' theory of possible persons, if at sometime in a creature's life a creature lacks a certain property, one can claim that the property is accidental. Thus, Scotus can, given his views about possible persons, claim that some properties are accidental to a creature. This solution would not, however, explain how all the properties we would intuitively think to be accidental to Socrates (or any other being) are accidental. Take, for instance, the property of having five fingers on the right hand. Socrates, as far as we know, had this property all through his life. Thus, having five fingers on his right hand during his entire life is an essential property of the identity of Socrates. But we would intuitively say that this is an accidental property of Socrates. Had Socrates slipped while carving a statue and lost his thumb, we would think that Socrates without the thumb was still Socrates. Yet, on Scotus' theory of possible persons, this does not seem to be the case. If Socrates at no time in his life lacked the property of having five fingers on his right hand, then having five fingers on his right hand would be essential and not accidental to Socrates. Thus, while a distinction between accidental and essential properties can be made out on Scotus' theory of possible persons, it does not fully explain why all the properties we would intuitively think to be accidental to a being are accidental. And there are even more serious difficulties with Scotus' analysis of omniscience.

According to Scotus, God knows what agents do because he knows what properties like "would turn right at Campus and University on April 19, 1986" constitute creatures. These creatures are free relative to some action, according to Scotus, if they have the ability to perform the action and the ability to refrain from performing the action and if they will the performance or the refraining in accordance with their natures. But this notion of freedom, given Scotus' views about possible persons, leads to some counter-intuitive conclusions. For example, we would say that, if a man were forced at gunpoint to rob a poor box on Christmas Day, 1984, he does not perform the action freely. Unfortunately, it would be a free action according to Scotus' definition of 'freedom'. The man would, of course, have the ability to rob from the poor box and to refrain from robbing it. Moreover, the man would be acting according to his nature since he acts in accordance with a property ("would rob a poor box while being forced at gunpoint on Christmas Day, 1984") that is an essential part of his being the person he is. Since Scotus identifies a person with the sum of the properties he possesses, seemingly all the actions a person performs are in accordance with the person's nature. Thus all the actions a person performs are free—even actions that are coerced.

Clearly, this is a serious difficulty for Scotus' theory of freedom, for we do not think that a person freely performs an action when he is forced to do so. In order to deal with this counter-intuitive result, Scotus must distinguish between a person's identity and a person's nature. Although he did not address this issue, he could perhaps distinguish a person's identity from a person's nature in this way: All the properties a person possesses can be seen as constituting the person's identity. On the other hand, those ways an agent acts if he is impeded by no other created agent would constitute a person's nature. Thus, if a person habitually steals from a poor box, we would say it is part of his nature to steal. On the other hand, if he generally refrains from stealing from the boxes, we would think it to be part of his nature not to steal.[2] Having made this distinction, Scotus could claim that freedom is judged relative to a person's nature and not his identity. While God may know what a creature does by knowing the properties constituting a creature's identity, a creature is free only if it acts in accordance with its nature.

There are perhaps difficulties with contrasting a person's identity and his nature, but Scotus' theory of freedom must include such a distinction on pain of generating very counter-intuitive results. This is not to say that his analysis of omniscience and his view of freedom would be incoherent without such a distinction, but only that without such a distinction his theories would have very counter-intuitive moral implications. In fact, the moral implications of Scotus' notion of freedom are even more serious. To see this, we need only to return to Leibniz's attempt to define 'freedom'.

Leibniz did not identify freedom and the liberty of spontaneity as Hobbes did because he thought that this definition would make beasts, as well as men, free. Leibniz therefore argued that freedom must consist of contingency, spontaneity, and intelligence. As we have seen, Leibniz took intelligence to be the ability to choose from a number of alternative actions. Unfortunately, as I argued earlier, since every person is determined by his complete, individual concept to choose only one course of action, there is no real choice among alternatives in the Leibnizian system and, consequently, Leibniz's notion of freedom is, in his own system, unrealizable.

Even though Leibniz's theory of freedom is inconsistent with his analysis of God's omniscience, he has uncovered a serious difficulty for anyone embracing something like the liberty of spontaneity: How does one separate unfree beasts from free agents? Presumably Scotus did not address this problem because he thought it obvious that beasts are not free since they are non-voluntary agents. Unfortunately, given Scotus' views about abilities, it is clear that beasts are not mere non-voluntary agents. For example, on one occasion a dog may attack a small boy; on another occasion it may be very friendly to the boy. This would indicate that the dog has the ability to perform an action and the ability to refrain from performing the same action. Since there must be possible dogs as well as possible persons and these possible dogs must be sets of properties that God chooses or does not choose to instantiate, dogs would act according to their identities and natures and thus be free according to Scotus' definition of 'freedom'. Clearly, Scotus' definition of 'freedom' must contain or presuppose something more than the two clauses we have seen; otherwise, it would render beasts as well as free agents free.

In order to assess responsibility for actions it is necessary to separate unfree beasts from free agents. Intuitively, it would make no sense to hold a beast like a raccoon responsible for stealing eggs from a hen house. This is something raccoons do and no amount of punishment or training will change this. On the other hand, holding a human being responsible for stealing and punishing him for theft does make sense. We think that the agent can mend his ways given sufficient inducements. So, our normal notions of responsibility and punishment seem to require a distinction between beasts and free agents. Any theory of freedom must make this distinction in order to succeed. Since Scotus' own theory fails to make such a distinction, it is to that extent inadequate.

Moreover, there are even more serious problems with Scotus' theory that are related to responsibility. On Scotus' analysis, men must do what they do since they must follow out their identities. God knows the make-up of the possible creatures he instantiates, and his choice determines what creatures there are as well as what activities they perform. As we have seen in the discussion of the free will defense, God could have chosen any number of men who would always freely do what is right. Yet, he chose many men who do wrong. Given Augustine's and Pike's remarks about God's possible reasons for thus ensuring evil, the existence of evil does not count against God's goodness. He might, after all, have a morally sufficient reason for creating men who do evil. Scotus probably would have endorsed this solution to the problem of evil. But there is a more serious question for Scotus—which is the same difficulty Erasmus pointed out about Luther's analysis of God's knowledge. If we grant that free agents who do wrong should be held responsible for their actions and be punished in this world or the next, then God, in choosing men who do evil, is choosing to create men he punishes. He could create people he rewards but instead chooses men he punishes. God thus appears to be a very reprehensible creator who relishes in constructing worlds in which men are guaranteed to suffer for what they must do. Moreover, there is something disturbing about even punishing creatures for what they must do. If a man is determined by the set of properties that constitute his essence to do what he does, why should he be punished for what he does?

These are some of the major objections that can be raised against Scotus' view of freedom and his analysis of God's omniscience. It is clear, I think, that the objections to the moral implications of Scotus' views constitute the most serious objections. Yet, it is important to emphasize that these same objections can be urged against any non-libertarian notion of freedom and, more specifically, against any theistic non-libertarian notion of freedom. These objections have in fact been raised against the theories of soft determinists and compatibilists since the time of Thomas Hobbes.

In response to these objections to the moral implications of a non-libertarian view of freedom, many contemporary compatibilists urge a restructuring of basic moral notions of reward, punishment, guilt, and so on. In fact, many have presented programs for revising these notions.[3] Whether these revisions should be accepted is a point of contention today. For example, many people argue that moral theories should fit, and not structure, our moral notions, and they reject the program of revisionists. It is, however, beyond the scope of this work to make any judgments about the debate. It is sufficient to note that the resolution of this debate will affect the proper assessment of Scotus' theory of omniscience. If a non-libertarian view of freedom is rejected as morally inadequate, Scotus' view of omniscience—as well as those of the other members of the voluntarist tradition—must be rejected. Importantly, rejection of Scotus' theory must be based on a rejection of the moral implications of the analysis. One cannot reject his analysis as inconsistent. Since Scotus embraces a non-libertarian notion of freedom, his analysis of God's omniscience is not inconsistent with his views about freedom.

Notes

CHAPTER 1

1. Cp. Nelson Pike, *God and Timelessness* (New York: Schocken Books, 1970), pp. 54f. Throughout my essay, I assume that God is essentially omniscient in Pike's sense of the notion.

2. In his article on the problem of future contingents for the *Cambridge History of Later Medieval Philosophy* (Cambridge: Cambridge University Press, 1982), Calvin Normore discusses the positions of these men.

3. He discusses the problem in the *Summa Theologiae, Summa Contra Gentiles, De Veritate,* and his *Commentary on the Sentences.* Anthony Kenny has discussed some of the complexities of Aquinas' views in *Aquinas: A Critical Collection* (Oxford: Clarendon Press, 1979), Chap. 5.

4. Cp. *De Veritate,* question 2, article 12, objection two.

5. This part of Aquinas' discussion is to be found in his reply to objection four.

6. This discussion is found in Aquinas' replies to objections five and six. See also *Summa Contra Gentiles,* I, chap. 67, 6.

7. This discussion is found in Aquinas' reply to objection four. The discussion is even more complicated than my presentation indicates since Aquinas also distinguishes between two components of God's foreknowledge: the act of foreknowing and the content of the foreknowledge. For the sake of simplicity, I have tried to eliminate as many complications as possible from my presentation.

8. Eleonore Stump and Norman Kretzmann in "Eternity" (*Journal of Philosophy,* 78 [August 1981], pp. 429–58) discuss the concept of eternity as advanced by Boethius and Aquinas. They discuss the relationship of 'being present to' between temporal entities and an eternal being on pp. 441–44.

9. Cp. *Summa Contra Gentiles,* I, chap. 66.

10. I have used the text of the question found in Appendix A to Volume 6 of the Vatican Critical Edition of Scotus' *Ordinatio* (Vatican City: Vatican Press, 1950 –). Another version of the question can be found in the *Lectura,* published in Volume XVII of the Vatican Critical Edition. Hermann Schwamm has summarized Scotus' various texts on the problem of God's omniscience in his *Das göttliche Vorherwissen bei Duns Scotus und seinen ersten Anhängern* (*Philosophie und Grenzwissenschaften,* Vo. Band – 1/4 Heft [Innsbruck: Felizian Rauch, 1934]), pp. 1–91. Many of the points Scotus raises in Book I, distinctions 38 and 39 can also be found in Book I, distinction 2, question 1.

11. Cp. the second reply to the fifth objection (*Ordinatio,* Vol. 6, pp. 440–41, Vatican Ed.).

12. Ibid., p. 438.

13. The essential order of causes is one of the chief topics of *De Primo Principio* (text presented and translated by Allan Wolter as *A Treatise on God as First Principle* [Chicago: Franciscan Herald Press, 1966]). See especially p. 84.

William Rowe in *The Cosmological Argument* (Princeton: Princeton University Press, 1975) has given an excellent characterization of an essential order on pp. 23ff.

14. *Treatise on God,* p. 85.

15. Cp. *Ordinatio,* Vol. 6, p. 415, Vatican Ed.

16. The account I present in these pages must be taken as inexact. One cannot think of the steps as literally sequential, for this would violate God's simplicity, a notion Scotus defends in several places: *Ordinatio* I, distinction 2, question 1; *Ordinatio* I, distinction 8, part 2, question unica; *Ordinatio* I, distinction 24. The steps are regarded by Scotus as a logical ordering occurring all at once in God's timelessness. They thus do not entail that God has temporal segments or that he changes. Stump and Kretzmann discuss the nature of atemporal willing in "Eternity," pp. 444–47.

17. That God has a contingent will does not conflict with either God's necessity or his simplicity. This has been argued for convincingly by William Mann in his article "Simplicity and Immutability in God" (*International Philosophical Quarterly,* 23 [1983], 267–76) in his replies to objections three and four. Some of the issues connected to divine simplicity in Scotus' writings are discussed by Marilyn Adams in "Ockham on Identity and Distinction" (*Franciscan Studies,* 14 [1976], 24–43). While I do not see any conflict between Scotus' analysis of God's omniscience and his views about God's simplicity, I hope to address this issue in detail in a future essay.

18. *Ordinatio,* Vol. 6, p. 407, Vatican Ed.

19. Ibid., p. 410 (translated by Marilyn Adams in an unpublished translation).

20. Anthony Kenny presents a similar argument in "Divine Fore-knowledge and Human Freedom," in *Aquinas: A Critical Collection,* pp. 262f. Etienne Gilson in *Jean Duns Scot: Introduction à Ses Positions Fondamentales* (Paris: J. Vrin, 1952) presents Scotus' argument on pp. 311f.

21. Stump and Kretzmann offer, I believe, the best explanation of this distinction in "Eternity," pp. 434ff. They specifically mention Aquinas' analogy in n. 18, p. 441.

22. Cp. *Ordinatio,* Book I, distinction 43, question unica, where Scotus equates "*x* is possible" and "*x* is in God's intellect in the first instant of nature." Scotus' notion of "instants of nature" is an explanatory device. He uses it to explain the logical ordering of an activity that either occurs outside time or occurs at one instant of time. In the case at hand, Scotus is describing what we would call the logical steps in God's willing the actual world. These steps, according to Scotus, occur outside time and so they cannot be temporally ordered. The first instant of nature is logically prior to the second instant of nature, and the second is logically prior to the third, and so on.

23. Gilson, in *Jean Duns Scot,* p. 310, discusses this argument as one of the three reasons Scotus opts for a voluntaristic analysis of God's omniscience.

24. Cp. *Summa Theologiae,* question 14, article 11, *responsio* and article 5.

25. Ibid., article 9, ad 3.

26. *Summa Contra Gentiles,* I, chaps. 50, 51, 52, 65, 66, and 68. Cp. Etienne Gilson, *The Philosophy of St. Thomas Aquinas* (St. Louis: B. Herder, 1939), pp. 195ff.

27. See, for example, *Summa Contra Gentiles,* Book I, chap. 66, and *Summa Theologiae,* Part I, question 14, article 9, and Part I, question 1, article 3, ad 2.

28. I am indebted to Joseph M. Incandela for my remarks on God's practical knowledge. See also Robert Leet Patterson, *The Conception of God in the Philosophy of Aquinas* (London: George Allen and Unwin, Ltd., 1933), pp. 307–19.

29. *Summa Contra Gentiles,* Book III, chap. 75.

30. There are students of Aquinas who think he holds that God does will the actions of free creatures, e.g., the predeterminators I treat in chapter four. Many attribute to Aquinas a compatibilist notion of freedom and would see great similarity between Aquinas and Scotus on God's knowledge and human freedom. See Patterson, *Conception of God,* pp. 347–48.

CHAPTER 2

1. For example, the following treat Book II, distinction 25: Lawrence Roberts, *Duns Scotus and the Concept of Human Freedom* (Diss. Indiana University, 1969); Bernardine Bonansea, "Duns Scotus' Voluntarism," *Studies in Philosophy and the History of Philosophy,* Vol.

4, John K. Ryan, ed. (Washington, D.C.: The Catholic University of America Press, 1965); and Carlo Balič, *Les Commentaires de Jean Duns Scot* (Louvain: Bureaux de la Revue, 1927) and "Une question inédite de J. Duns Scot sur la Volonté," *Recherches de Théologie Ancienne et Médiévale,* Vol. 3 (Louvain, 1931). Simo Knuuttila in "Time and Modality in Scholasticism," *Reforging the Great Chain of Being,* S. Knuuttila, ed. (Netherlands: D. Reidel, 1980) and Arthur Falk in "The Forebearance of an Instantaneous Angel: Time, Possibility and Free Will," *Modern Schoolman,* 61 (January 1984), pp. 101–16, discuss sections of *Ordinatio* I, distinctions 38 and 39.

2. *Ordinatio* I, distinction 1, part 2, question 1 (Vatican Ed., Vol. 2, p. 50).

3. Ibid., question 2, p. 66.

4. Ibid., p. 99, and *Opus Oxonensis,* Book II, distinction 7, question unica (Vivès Ed., Vol. 12, p. 377a [Paris: Vivès, 1894]). Hereafter, I shall refer to this version of his sentence commentary as *Oxon.*

5. *Oxon.* III, distinction 17, question unica (Vivès, Vol. 14, p. 652b f.).

6. Ibid., p. 652b: ... quia omnis voluntas est domina sui actus ... and p. 654b, n. 4: Ad primum principale concedo majoram, quod omnis voluntas est domina sui actus.

7. Ibid., p. 654b, n. 3: ... dicitur autem libera, inquantum in potestate ejus est, ita elicere actum oppositum inclinationi, sicut conformem, et non elicere, sicut elicere.

8. *Oxon.* II, distinction 33, question unica, n. 2 (Vivès, Vol. 15, p. 439a): ... quia voluntas cum sit libera, potest sufficienter se determinare ...

9. Ibid., p. 442a: ... voluntas est indeterminata, non tantum ad opposita, sed etiam in modo agendi, scilicet recte et non recte.

10. *Oxon.* IV, distinction 43, question 4 (Vivès, Vol. 20, p. 113a).

11. *Oxon.* IV, distinction 49, question 10 (Vivès, Vol. 21, pp. 317b f.).

12. *De Primo Principio,* p. 93.

13. *Ordinatio* I, distinction 38, part 2, and distinction 39, questions 1–5 (Vatican Ed., Vol. 6, p. 417).

14. An overweight person who tries to be slim but never succeeds because of chronic overeating would be an example of the distinction.

15. Scotus claims this in *Ordinatio* I, distinction 38, part 2, and distinction 39, questions 1–5 (Vatican Ed., Vol. 6, pp. 426f.).

16. Ibid., p. 417.

17. Ibid.: Tamen est et alia (non ita manifesta), absque omni successione.

18. Ibid., p. 418: ... ita ponit illum in esse—tanquam effectum suum contingentem—quod ut prior naturaliter, posset aeque ponere aliud oppositum in esse.

Simo Knuuttila in "Time and Modality in Scholasticism," pp. 217f. discusses Scotus' views about the not-so-evident power as well as some of Scotus' views about modalities. Knuuttila's work is interesting and impressive. I believe that he is mistaken in assuming that Scotus' definition of 'freedom' is simply the ability to cause or refrain from causing.

19. Vatican Ed., Vol. 6, p. 419: . . . sed quarta non concomitatur istam—scilicet ad opposita simul—quia illa nulla est.

20. Ibid., p. 418: Et ista potentia, realis, est potentia prioris naturaliter (ut actus primi) ad opposita quae sunt posteriora naturaliter (ut actus secundi).

21. Ockham criticizes Scotus' instants of nature in his *Tractatus de praedestinatione et de praescientia Dei et de futuris contingentibus* in *Opera Philosophica,* Vol. 2 (St. Bonaventure, N.Y.: Franciscan Institute, 1978), pp. 533–36. A translation of this work is published as *Predestination, God's Foreknowledge and Future Contingents,* Marilyn Adams and Norman Kretzmann, trans. (New York: Meredith Corporation, 1969), pp. 72–73. Scotus also uses the notion of instants of nature to explain how, for whatever God wills, he could will something else (cp. Vatican Ed., Vol. 6, pp. 425f.). Norman Kretzmann ("Continuity, Contrareity, Contradiction, and Change") and Paul Spade ("Quasi-Aristotelianism") in *Infinity and Continuity in Ancient and Medieval Thought,* N. Kretzmann, ed. (Ithaca: Cornell University Press, 1982) discuss Scotus' instants of nature and their appropriation by the Quasi-Aristotelians to solve perceived difficulties in Aristotle's analysis of instantaneous change.

22. Vatican Ed., Vol. 6; p. 418: Hanc etiam potentiam realem activam (priorem naturaliter ipso quod producit) concomitatur potentia logica, quae est non-repugnantia terminorum.

23. Ibid., p. 419.

24. I am indebted to Nelson Pike for pointing out Scotus' non-standard use of 'power'.

25. Knuuttila discusses these objections on pp. 228ff in "Time and Modality in Scholasticism."

26. Vatican Ed., Vol. 6, p. 427.

27. Scotus' argument is implied in this passage (Vatican Ed., Vol. 6, p. 418): . . . non enim modo [voluntas] est contingens causa quia praeexistebat ante istud instans in quo causat (et tunc 'ut praeexistens' causare vel non causare). . . . In this passage, Scotus indicates that his principal inclination in determining whether an agent is free or not is to see if the agent could have at a prior instant done otherwise than he did.

28. Balič, *Les Commentaires* and "Une question inédite."

29. *Studies in Philosophy,* Vol. 4.

30. *John Duns Scotus and the Concept of Human Freedom* is Roberts' unpublished doctoral dissertation while "John Duns Scotus and the Concept of Human Freedom" is an article based on the dissertation that appeared in *Ad Mentem I. Duns Scoti* (Rome: Scotist Commission, 1972). Hereafter, I refer to the doctoral dissertation as Roberts I and to the article as Roberts II.

31. Cp. Bonansea, "Duns Scotus' Voluntarism," pp. 100f., and Balič, *Les Commentaires,* pp. 289f., and "Une question inédite," pp. 198f. John Wippel in *The Metaphysical Thought of Godfrey of Fontaines: A Study in Late Thirteenth-Century Philosophy* (Washington, D.C.: The

Catholic University of America Press, 1981) discusses Godfrey's position on pp. 194–202.

32. Cp. Bonansea, "Duns Scotus' Voluntarism," pp. 102f.; Balič, *Les Commentaires,* pp. 267f., and "Une question inédite," pp. 195f.

33. Balič, *Les Commentaires,* pp. 277f., and "Une question inédite," pp. 199f.

34. Cp. Roberts II, pp. 322f.

35. Balič, "Une question inédite," p. 203: ... voluntas tamen est causa principalior ...

36. Roberts I, p. 41.

37. Balič, "Une question inédite," p. 193. Roberts in Roberts I, pp. 76f., criticizes the plausibility of the case.

38. In Roberts I, Roberts attributes to Scotus this definition of 'freedom': An agent is free as regards *x* if and only if the agent can do *x* and can do the contrary of *x*. He regards this as a libertarian definition in Roberts I, pp. 54, 108, and 161. He also affirms Scotus' libertarianism in his "The Contemporary Relevance of Duns Scotus' Doctrine of Human Freedom" in *Regnum Hominis et Regnum Dei: Acta Quarti Congressus Scotistici Internationales,* Studia-Scotistica 6, (Rome: Societas Internationales Scotistica, 1978), p. 536.

39. Anthony Kenny, in his *Will, Freedom and Power* (London: Blackwell, 1975), offers this as a compatibilist definition of 'freedom'. He thinks that this definition is compatible with determinism only because in chapters seven and eight he dismisses psychological determinism. Without this assumption I think the definition is incompatible with determinism and is a fitting definition of 'libertarianism'.

40. Roberts I, pp. 258–59. The Latin text is given in Balič, *Les Commentaires,* p. 299.

CHAPTER 3

1. Vivès, Vol. 21, pp. 180–271. In the Wadding edition, the text is given as question four rather than as question six.

2. Robert Prentice in his article "The Degree and Mode of Liberty in the Beatitude of the Blessed," *Ad Mentem I. Duns Scoti,* discusses these points on pp. 332–37.

3. In his discussion of Anselm's views about the will and freedom in *Anselm's Doctrine of Freedom and the Will* (Lewiston, N.Y.: The Edwin Mellen Press, 1981) and "Anselm's Definition of Freedom" (*Religious Studies,* 9 [1973], pp. 297–306) Stanley Kane discusses Anselm's definition of 'freedom'—"Freedom is the ability to keep the rectitude of the will for its own sake (*Anselm's Doctrine,* p. 129)—and presents Anselm's solution to a case similar to the one Scotus discusses (ibid., pp. 83–84). In his *Man and His Approach to God in John Duns Scotus* (Boston: University Press of America, 1983), p. 61, Bernardine Bonansea claims that Scotus makes Anselm's definition of 'freedom' his own. Bonansea cites three texts to support his view, but a careful consideration of these texts indicates that Scotus is not endorsing Anselm's definition but is using it to discuss issues related to univocity and the simple perfections.

4. Vivès, Vol. 21, p. 232, n. 13.

5. Ibid., p. 233b:... sed non repugnat sibi, quod contingentia ejus non ponat contingentiam ex parte effectus simpliciter, quantum ex parte causae superioris, quia causa superior non determinatur ab ipsa; non est ergo simpliciter contra naturam ejus, quod determinetur a causa superiori, hoc est, quod non sit contra naturam ejus oppositum agere, sicut esset contra naturam ejus determinati ab habitu, sive a natura inferiori.

6. I do not see why, in most cases, a superior agent could not also determine by constraining the nature of inferior agents. Perhaps Scotus also accepts this and merely wants to claim that, as a matter of fact, superior agents (and especially God) do not determine in this way.

7. Cp. Vivès, Vol. 21, p. 229a.

8. Kenny, in his *Will, Freedom, and Power,* spends a great amount of time making this distinction clear. Kane in his *Anselm's Doctrine of Freedom and the Will* discusses Anselm's views on opportunity on p. 130f. and his views on abilities on p. 142f. There are similarities between the views of Anselm and Scotus on these matters.

9. Allan B. Wolter and Felix Alluntis have translated the *Quodlibetal Questions* as *God and Creatures: The Quodlibetal Questions* (Princeton: Princeton University Press, 1975). The Latin text is found in volumes 25 and 26 of the Vivès edition.

10. *God and Creatures,* p. 369 (Vivès, Vol. 26, p. 180).

11. Ibid., p. 370.

12. This is Wolter and Alluntis's (pp. 376–77) rendering of Vivès, Vol. 26, p. 190, n. 7.

13. Ibid.

14. Wolter and Alluntis's (p. 377) rendering of Vivès, Vol. 26, p. 190. When Scotus uses the term 'quodcumque creatum' in the Latin text, which Wolter and Alluntis translate as 'creature', he means any created thing. This includes the will as well as the acts of the will. I assume that God's determining that certain volitions exist in a creature's will is tantamount to his determining the creature's will.

15. Cp. p. 37 above.

16. Wolter and Alluntis's (p. 406) rendering of Vivès, Vol. 26, p. 241b.

17. Vivès, Vol. 13, p. 221b: Dico ergo ad quaestionem quod nihil aliud a voluntate est causa totalis volitionis in voluntate. Una ratio praeter praedictas est ista: aliquid evenit in rebus contingenter: et voco contingenter evenire, evitabiliter evenire.

Les Commentaires, p. 299: Respondeo ergo ad questionem, quod nihil aliud a voluntate potest esse totalis causa volitionis in voluntate secundum quod voluntas determinat se libere ad actum volendi causandum. Quod probo sic: supposito quod aliquid contingenter evenit in rebus ita quod pro illo instanti pro quo evenit potest non evenire, ut sic evitabiliter eveniat...

18. *De Primo Principio,* p. 83: Item tertio sic: aliquid causatur contingenter; ergo prima causa contingenter causat; igitur volens causat.

19. *Quodlibetal Questions,* number 18: *God and Creatures,* p. 407 and p. 416 (Vivès, Vol. 26, p. 242 and pp. 257–258).

20. Robert Grosseteste does make the claim in his *De Libero Arbitrio,* chapter 6. In fact, Scotus in *Ordinatio* I, distinction 1, question 2 (Vatican Ed., Vol. 2, p. 88, n. 131) separates freedom from mere contingency: " 'libere' vero non infert 'contingenter'." This is further emphasized in an interpolated text to this passage cited by the editors of the Vatican edition: "Contra, 'naturaliter' et 'contingenter' non inferunt 'libere' sicut inferiora suum superius."

21. Wolter and Alluntis's (pp. 384–85) rendering of Vivès, Vol. 26, p. 199a.

22. Wolter and Alluntis's (p. 385) rendering of Vivès, Vol. 26, p. 199b.

23. Vatican Ed., Vol. 6, pp. 336f.

24. Ibid., pp. 381f.

25. Unfortunately, in his analysis of the perpetuity of the beatific vision, he seems to allow that the blessed would be free even if forced by God to enjoy the vision. For this reason, I think his discussion of the question is ultimately inadequate even though it reveals many aspects of Scotus' view of freedom.

26. Wolter and Alluntis's (p. 387) rendering of Vivès, Vol. 26, p. 201.

CHAPTER 4

1. *Tractatus de praedestinatione,* pp. 517–18 (*Predestination,* pp. 72–73). See chap. 2, n. 21.

The various followers of Scotus are treated in Konstantz Michalski's "Le Problème de la volonté à Oxford et à Paris au XIVe siècle" in *Studia Philosophica,* Vol. 2 (Leopli: 1937), pp. 294f. Herman Schwamm also treats a number of Scotus' followers in his *Das göttliche Vorherwissen bei Duns Scotus und seinen ersten Anhängern.*

2. I have used the translation of J. I. Packer and O. R. Johnston (Westwood, N.J.: Fleming H. Revell, 1957).

3. I have used the translation of E. Gordon Rupp printed in Vol. 17 of the *Library of Christian Classics* (Philadelphia: Westminster Press, 1969).

4. Ibid., p. 66.

5. Luther, p. 81.

6. See p. 45 above.

7. Luther, p. 81 and p. 103.

8. Erasmus, p. 88.

9. Luther, p. 317.

10. I have used the translation of Henry Beveridge, 2 vols. (Grand Rapids, Michigan: Eerdmans Publishing Co., 1979).

11. Ibid., Vol. 1, p. 181.

12. Ibid., Vol. 1, p. 228 and pp. 254–55.

13. Ibid. On pp. 256–57 Calvin discusses Augustine. On p. 229 he eschews the term 'free will'.

14. Ibid., p. 205.

15. For the *Concordia* I have used the Antwerp edition of Joachim Trognaesius printed in 1595. I have used Dr. Friedrich Stegmuller's edition of the text of *De Scientia Dei* published in *Beitrage Zur Geschichte*

Der Philosophie Und Theologie Des Mittelalters, Band XXXII (Münster: Aschendorffschen, 1935).

16. *Concordia,* p. 227 (Quaestionis XIV, Articulis XIII, Disputatio LII).

17. *De Scientia,* p. 227. Cp. Matthew 11:21. Molina also appeals to the story of David and the citizens of Keilah (Samuel I, 23: 1–14), but he does not appeal to this story as frequently as he appeals to the story of Chorazin and Betsaida.

18. Gerard Smith in *Freedom in Molina* (Chicago: Loyola University Press, 1966) frequently suggests that Molina failed to understand Aquinas. Smith claims that part of Molina's difficulty came from understanding Aquinas through the explanations of Bañes; cp. p. 114 of *Freedom in Molina.*

19. *De Scientia,* p. 219.

20. Ibid., p. 241.

21. Ibid., p. 216.

22. Ibid.

23. Cp. p. 17 above.

24. *De Scientia,* pp. 220f.

25. Ibid., p. 220.

26. Ibid.

27. Ibid., p. 222.

28. Ibid., p. 223.

29. Ibid., p. 224.

30. Ibid., pp. 225f. In an unpublished paper, "God's Present and Ours: Buridan and De Molina on the Present Tense," Calvin Normore suggests that there are basic similarities between Molina's and Buridan's analysis of the eternal now. Both men work out elaborate rules for determining truth values of sentences pertaining to the eternal now that preserve both the principle of noncontradiction and the principle of bivalence.

31. *De Scientia,* pp. 232f.

32. Ibid.

33. Ibid., p. 234.

34. *Concordia,* p. 145, Quaestionis XIV, Articulis XIII, Disputatio XXXV.

35. *Concordia,* p. 234, Quaestionis XIV, Articulis XIII, Disputatio LII.

36. Ibid., p. 235.

37. *De Scientia,* pp. 209–13.

38. Ibid., pp. 226f.

39. Ibid. Molina's argument bears some similarity to what I describe in chapter one as Scotus' second argument against Aquinas.

40. Ibid., p. 227.

41. Ibid.

42. Ibid., p. 207.

43. Ibid.

44. As we have seen, Lawrence Roberts affirms this, as does Gerald Smith in his *Freedom in Molina.* Anton Pegis also claims this in his "Molina and Human Liberty" in *Jesuit Thinkers of the Renaissance,*

Gerald Smith, ed. (Milwaukee: Marquette University Press, 1939), p. 129. Gilson in his *Spirit of Medieval Philosophy* (New York: Scribner's, 1940), Chap. 15, especially pp. 321ff., briefly discusses Molina's relationship to the Protestant reformers and his debt to Scotus and Aquinas. Gilson also assumes that Scotus subscribes to a liberty of indifference. There are other mistakes in Gilson's presentation, but space prevents a full treatment of these.

45. *American Philosophical Quarterly,* 14 (April 1977), pp. 109ff.
46. Ibid., p. 111.
47. Ibid.
48. Ibid., pp. 111–12.
49. Ibid., p. 111.
50. Ibid., pp. 112–14.
51. My discussion in this paragraph of the text is heavily influenced by Nelson Pike's "Divine Omniscience and Voluntary Action," *Philosophical Review,* 74 (1965), pp. 27–46, and his *God and Timelessness,* pp. 53–86. I do assume, of course, that Molina thinks God is essentially omniscient.
52. Alvin Plantinga, *God, Freedom, and Evil* (New York: Harper and Row, 1974) pp. 65–73.
53. See John Turk Sander's "Of God and Freedom," *Philosophical Review,* 75 (1966), 219–25; Nelson Pike's reply to Sanders, "Of God and Freedom: A Rejoinder," *Philosophical Review,* 75 (1966), 369–79; Marilyn Adams's "Is the Existence of God a 'Hard' Fact?" *Philosophical Review,* 76 (1967), 492–503; and William Rowe's *Philosophy of Religion* (Encino: Dickenson Press, 1976), pp. 158–61 and "On Divine Foreknowledge and Human Freedom: A Reply," *Philosophical Studies,* 37 (1980), 429–30.

CHAPTER 5

1. G. W. Leibniz, *Theodicy: Essays on the Goodness of God, the Freedom of Man, and the Origin of Evil,* E. M. Huggard, trans. (New Haven: Yale University Press, 1952), p. 168. I refer to the body of the text according to paragraphs. Page references indicate material in addition to the text that is contained in the Huggard translation.
2. *The English Works of Thomas Hobbes* (London: John Bohn, 1841; 2nd reprint, Darmstadt, Germany: Scientia Verlag, 1966), Vol. 4.
3. Ibid., Vol. 5. The treatise appeared in 1656.
4. Ibid., Vol. 4, pp. 232–34. Vol. 5, p. 266.
5. Ibid., Vol. 4, p. 275.
6. Ibid., p. 239.
7. Ibid., p. 278.
8. Ibid., p. 273.
9. Ibid.
10. Leroy E. Lomeker, *Gottfried Wilhelm Leibniz: Philosophical Papers and Letters* (Chicago: The University of Chicago Press, 1956), pp. 7–17.
11. *Theodicy,* par. 1.
12. Ibid., pars. 39 and 40.

13. Ibid., par. 41.

14. Ibid., par. 46.

15. Cp. G. H. Parkinson in his *Leibniz on Human Freedom* in *Studia Leibnitiana*, Sonderheft 2 (Weisbaden: Franz Steiner Verlag GMBH, 1970), p. 49.

16. *Theodicy*, par. 47.

17. Ibid., par. 54.

18. Ibid., par. 42.

19. Of course, events subsequent to Saul's action would also be different. Alvin Plantinga in *The Nature of Necessity* (Oxford: Oxford University Press, 1974), pp. 44–69, describes what is meant by a 'possible world'.

20. *Theodicy*, par. 42.

21. Ibid., par. 43.

22. For example, in his letter of May 1686 printed in *Leibniz: Discourse on Metaphysics, Correspondence with Arnauld, Monadology* (Chicago: Open Court Publishing Co., 1902) pp. 103f., and in *The Leibniz-Arnauld Correspondence* (Manchester: Manchester University Press, 1967), pp. 24f.

23. *Theodicy*, p. 80.

24. Ibid., par. 132.

25. Ibid., par. 337.

26. Ibid., p. 383.

27. *Leibniz: Philosophical Writings*, G. H. Parkinson, ed. (London: J. M. Dent, 1973), p. 244, fn. e.

28. *Theodicy*, par. 52.

29. *Discourse on Metaphysics*, p. 69.

30. Ibid., p. 73.

31. Ibid.

32. Ibid., p. 125.

33. This is at least one reading of Augustine's remarks in *On Free Choice of the Will*, Book III, chaps. 2–4.

34. For example, *Theodicy*, par. 37 and p. 273. Also compare Parkinson's remark in *Leibniz: Philosophical Writings*, p. 24.

35. *Discourse on Metaphysics*, p. 90.

36. *Theodicy*, pars. 59 and 65.

37. Ibid., pars. 290 and 301.

38. *Discourse on Metaphysics*, pp. 48f.

39. In paragraph 75 he calls liberty of spontaneity "imperfect freedom."

40. *Theodicy*, pp. 393–404. In Hobbes' exchange with Dr. Bramhall, Dr. Bramhall often criticizes Hobbes' notion of freedom because it makes rivers and dumb beasts free (Vol. 4, p. 244; Vol. 5, p. 66 and p. 394). Hobbes' distinction between liberty and liberty of spontaneity shows that natural agents like rivers are not free. It does not, however, show how dumb beasts are not to be considered free agents.

41. Ibid., p. 396.

42. *Leibniz: Philosophical Writings*, p. 41 and p. 143; *Theodicy*, p. 396.

43. *Leibniz: Philosophical Writings*, p. 106.

44. Ibid., p. 107.

45. John Hostler, *Leibniz's Moral Philosophy* (London: Gerald Duckworth & Co., Ltd., 1975), p. 45.

46. Ibid., p. 46.

47. For example, Parkinson in *Leibniz on Human Freedom,* p. 60, and A. Burms and H. De Dijin in "Freedom and Logical Contingency in Leibniz" in *Studia Leibnitiana,* Band XI, 1979.

48. Hostler, p. 34.

49. *Discourse on Metaphysics,* p. 40.

50. Cp. Alvin Plantinga's *The Nature of Necessity,* p. 88.

51. David Lewis defends Leibniz's theories about possible worlds in his "Counterpart Theory and Quantified Modal Logic," *Journal of Philosophy,* 65 (1968), p. 113. Alvin Plantinga attacks Leibniz's views in his "Transworld Identity or Worldbound Individuals?" in Michael Loux, ed., *The Possible and the Actual* (Ithaca: Cornell Univ. Press, 1979). Robert Adams comments on Leibniz's views in his "Theories of Actuality" in *The Possible and the Actual.*

52. Hostler, pp. 38–41.

53. Ibid., p. 35.

CHAPTER 6

1. Prior talks about problems surrounding omniscience in his "The Formalities of Omniscience" (*Philosophy,* 37, 1962).

2. Alvin Plantinga, *God and Other Minds* (Ithaca: Cornell University Press, 1967); *God, Freedom, and Evil;* and *Nature of Necessity.* Pike's responses are: "Plantinga on the Free Will Defence: A Reply," *Journal of Philosophy,* 62 (1966), pp. 93–104, and "Plantinga on Free Will and Evil," *Religious Studies,* 15 (December 1979), pp. 449–73.

3. *Nature of Necessity,* p. 165.

4. *God, Freedom, and Evil,* p. 35.

5. Ibid., p. 54.

6. Ibid., p. 40.

7. Ibid., p. 41.

8. Both (23) and (24) are counterfactuals and Plantinga gives a brief treatment of the logic of counterfactuals in *The Nature of Necessity,* pp. 174–80. One might think that, given that (23) is in fact true in the actual world, (24) cannot be true in any possible world. This is a mistake, however; the possible worlds in which (24) is true might not be as similar to the actual world as the possible but unactual worlds in which (23) is true, but there are such possible worlds.

9. Plantinga's most explicit treatment of omnipotence is in *God and Other Minds,* pp. 136ff. His definition bears great similarity to points Scotus makes in *Ordinatio* I, distinction 43.

10. *God, Freedom, and Evil,* pp. 45f.

11. Of course, Plantinga would be correct in maintaining that God *as he exists in our actual world* [subject to the truth of (32)] cannot bring about W^g. But this is beside the point as I argued in relation to the aardvark case. Instead of actualizing our actual world and subjecting himself to the restrictions of this world [among others, the truth of (32)], God could have actualized W^g and could have subjected himself

to a different set of restrictions [among others, the truth of (32)]. The important question is then: Why is W^g not the actual world?

12. *God, Freedom, and Evil,* p. 47.

13. Ibid., p. 48.

14. Ibid., p. 46.

15. Ibid., p. 49.

16. *God, Freedom, and Evil,* pp. 49–51, and *The Nature of Necessity,* chap. 4, secs. 10–12.

17. *God, Freedom, and Evil,* p. 51.

18. It seems unnecessary to summarize the argument here. The interested reader can examine it on p. 52 of *God, Freedom, and Evil.*

19. Ibid., pp. 52–53.

20. This is true both for the formulation in *God, Freedom, and Evil* and for the formulation in *The Nature of Necessity,* p. 188.

21. "Plantinga on Free Will and Evil," pp. 460–61. I see my argument in this chapter as closely related to elements of the argument Pike offers in his essay.

22. Cp. Plantinga's remarks in *The Nature of Necessity,* p. 169, and *God, Freedom, and Evil,* pp. 38–39.

23. *God, Freedom, and Evil,* p. 45.

24. "Plantinga on Free Will and Evil," pp. 467f. In his article, Pike discusses God as if he were in time and my discussion reflects this assumption.

25. Adams, "Middle Knowledge and the Problem of Evil," is discussed by Pike in "Plantinga on Free Will and Evil," pp. 467–69.

26. "Plantinga on Free Will and Evil," p. 468.

27. Mackie and McCloskey both discuss this point in their essays in *God and Evil* (Englewood Cliffs, N.J.: Prentice Hall, 1964).

28. It has been suggested to me that God could make *a priori* probabilistic prediction. That is, he could assign probabilities to actions independently of there being any data upon which to determine probabilities. It is difficult for me to understand what this would be like, however, and I consequently adopt a Humean view of probability.

29. There is much unclarity in the phrase "significant interference." How much interference is significant and thus a breach of a person's freedom? I have no ready answer to this question, but I do not think this failure undermines the point of this section.

30. "Plantinga on Free Will and Evil," pp. 471–72.

31. "Hume on Evil," in *God and Evil.*

32. "Plantinga on Free Will and Evil," p. 467.

33. In his "Plantinga on Free Will and Evil," pp. 460–61, Pike connects his Edam story with Leibniz's notion of "fulguration". Pike assumes in his Edam story, as Leibniz does in his account of God's knowledge, that what God instantiates is, as it were, ready-made. He does not create the various Edam-variations. As logical possibilities, they are present to him without any activity on his part. God merely allows some possible Edam-variation to become actual by instantiating it rather than some other.

34. Cp. J. Lucas in his *The Freedom of the Will* (Oxford: Oxford University Press, 1970).

CHAPTER 7

1. Cp. Parkinson, *Leibniz: Philosophical Writings,* p. xiv.

2. C. A. Campbell in his "Is 'Freewill' a Pseudo-Problem?" *Mind,* 60, no. 240 (October 1951) [reprinted in part in *Free Will and Determinism,* Bernard Berofsky, ed. (New York: Harper and Row, 1966)] argues that libertarianism requires a distinction between an act being of a person and an act being of a person's character. While Campbell is not writing with Scotus' views in mind, his article perhaps provides a start for separating Scotus' notions of a person's identity and a person's nature.

3. Moritz Schlick in his "When Is A Man Responsible?" (reprinted in part in *Free Will and Determinism*) argues for reassessing our notion of responsibility. Richard Brandt in his "Determinism and the Justifiability of Moral Blame," in *Determinism and Freedom In the Age of Modern Science,* Sidney Hook, ed. (New York: Macmillan, 1970) talks about the relationship of determinism to moral responsibility, praise, blame, duty, and obligation. Elizabeth Beardsley in "Determinism and Moral Perspectives" (*Philosophy and Phenomenological Research,* Vol. 21, 1960) goes further than most compatibilists in asserting a program for assessing praise and blame within a compatibilist framework.

Index